Marketing Apps & Selling Apps

How to Create, Sell and Market Apps.

App Development, Costs, Tools, Tips, Planning
and Promoting Your App.

By

Albert Luton

Table of Contents

General Introduction

Our age can best be described as the age of information and communication technology made possible by the use of computer and mobile devices in the doing of businesses and other economic activities. The effectiveness and efficiency of computers are derived from software and apps running on them. This is because virtually every operation carried out through these devices is executed with an app, software or a program. As computing in general and mobile computing in particular are rising, the app industries are booming. In other words, computers and mobile devices can be likened to empty cases if no applications and software are installed in them. This highlights the importance of application development in our era.

If you know how to create, market, popularize and sell an app, definitely, you are going to make a lot of money from it. Though app creation requires a basic programming knowledge, it is not a difficult task left for the exceptionally talented people. If you are determined and you are passionate about app development and marketing, there is no doubt that you are going to make a good sum of money from it.

The content of this book is borne out of many years of practical experience and research. The tips given have survived the test of time. If you get them correct as explained herein, it is a matter of time until you become a pro in the marketing and selling of apps. Note that though an attempt is made to explain what apps are and how to create one, the crux of the book is the marketing and selling hints provided. In other words, you will require another book if you have no knowledge of programming or app development.

Chapter 1. Applications: The Basics

The word app or application has become a very common word in the world today, especially with the rise in mobile devices and use of computers. There are very few people using these communication devices who have not heard of it or that don't use it or own one app. But the truth is only a few people know exactly what apps are and how they differ from software and programs. In this first chapter of the book, I am going to explain what an app is, its types and how it differs from software and programs. There are some people that will want to go into app development but they are not sure whether it is a profitable venture or not. I am also going to explain the profitability of such an engagement as well as debunk various myths circulating the Internet about apps in general and the marketing and selling of apps. Let's start our discussion by explaining what an app is.

Understanding What Apps Are

The term app is a shortened word for application. It refers to any computer-based program or software designed to be used for the execution of a specific or group of coordinated operations, activities, functions or tasks. Some apps are web-based, meaning that they are operated via a web browser. However, there are other types of apps that can be run through electronic devices as well as mobile devices like Smartphones, Tablets, iPads and iPhones. Some applications are designed to be used with the Internet while some do not require any connection to the Internet. They can be operated offline on a computerized device. Typical examples of apps are spreadsheets, media players, photo editors, console games, web browsers, accounting applications and others.

There are several ways in which application developers publish them. Some apps are created and released as separate programs, while some are incorporated into computer system software. They can be published to be compatible with one or a number of operating systems while some are made to run on various operation systems. Regardless of how an application is designed, its purpose is always to help a user carry out a specific activity. This is where an application differs from software, programs, utility and programming tools. I shall differentiate between these terms later in this chapter.

In the computer and information technology field, there is what is known as a killer app. The major difference between these and other kinds of applications is that a killer app is only compatible with a platform. The essence of such a design is to make the app more desirable in the market. For example, Blackberry has email software that can only work on that platform and this helps to increase its popularity.

Apps are also known as end-user programs or productivity programs. The reason for this is quite obvious. Each application helps a user to execute particular functions like the sending of emails, carrying out research online, graphic design and many more. Put differently, it cannot carry out any other task outside the one it is designed to execute. Some are complex in their design, while some have a simple outlook. For example, word processing application software comes with default settings like the font size, margins, line spacing and the rest, but you will be able to adjust them to suit your requirements. With this app, you can edit your document adding pictures, colors, headings, etc. It also comes with functions like delete, move, copy, cut and many others. On the other hand, a calculator application is quite simple and may not require further settings.

There are different ways of obtaining and using apps. You can download and install them on your mobile device or computers. Alternatively, they can be stored on the cloud and used with any device that is connected to the Internet.

Mobile devices normally come with platforms such as Google Play Store, App Store, Appstore for Android and iTunes (depending on the type of device) where users can enter to download apps. Some are offered at a fee while some are available free of charge. In the case of desktop apps, one can obtain them through official and unofficial sources. Examples of official sources are Window Store for apps that are compatible with Window operating system and Mac App Store for those that are meant to run on Mac OS. Unofficial sources are FileHippo.com and Softpedia.

Types of Apps

Apps are available in different types. It can be distinguished based on the platform they are used on and also based on the functions they are meant to serve. Before going into the various classifications of apps, I would like to mention that nowadays, the shortened word "app" is used in reference to mobile device applications such as apps for tablets, smartphones, iPod, iPad and iPhones in contradistinction from PCs applications. However, there are also some people that refer to desktop applications as apps.

Classification based on platforms
Under this classification, we have the following:

Native apps
These refer to apps that are designed exclusively for a particular mobile operating system (OS). This means that they cannot function in any other OS outside the one it is compatible with. For this reason, they are called native apps because they are like "citizens" or "locals" of a specific device or system. For example, you cannot make use of an app created for Blackberry on Symbian or one created for Symbian on Blackberry. Similarly, systems such as Android, iOS, Windows phone and others have apps that are native to them.

Such applications have their strengths and drawbacks not just for developers but also for users. On the positive side, they normally perform excellently when compared to other kinds of apps. This is because their developers make use of the native device UI in creating them. Thus, their users get a impressive and rewarding experience. They are normally available in the app stores of their respective platform, meaning that users of these devices will not have any problem in accessing and downloading them. Developers of such apps make quick and more sales because they reach to their target audience quite easily. With them, a wide range of Application Programming Interfaces (APIs) can be accessed by users. These APIs do not in any way limit the use of the apps.

On the negative side, they are more expensive both for the developers and users. For the developers, they have to create one app in various forms with each being compatible with only one platform. If you have just one version, users of other types of operating system will not be able to access them. Having different forms of an app comes with added tasks for the developer. They have to create different support services for each variant. The same thing applies to their maintenance. The total cost incurred by their makers in creating and maintaining them will make the selling price higher.

Hybrid apps

Hybrid apps are those applications that are created to run on multiple operating systems. Once developed and released, users of any platform can use them. Their developers use multi-platform web technologies such as CSS, Javascript and HTML5 in creating them. They also give some benefits to users and developers, but they are not flawless. When compared to native apps, developers find it much easier and quicker to make them, as they use just one code base for all. The use of one code for all operating systems comes with other advantages: it makes maintenance to be more affordable and updates easier and smoother. APIs such as geolocation, accelerometer and gyroscope, which are widely used, are available here.

One of the downsides of these apps is that they are not as efficient as the native apps in performance, overall optimization and speed. In some instances, the apps do not have the same design and appearance in different platforms and this also causes some design issues. It may look great in a device but bad in another one.

Web apps

As the name implies, web applications are designed to operate with a browser, meaning that you need Internet connection to run them. They are similar in certain respect to native apps. Normally, they are written in CSS, JavaScript and HTML5. Usually, they take a user to a URL. Users can bookmark them and this serves as their install option. As a rule, these applications need a device's minimum memory to run.

One good thing about these types of apps is that one can access them from any device that is connected to the Internet. This is because personal details used in registering with them are stored in a server. Though this gives them an edge over other kinds of apps from a certain point of view, it can also turn out to be a disadvantage when one does not have a strong and efficient Internet connection. User experience with poor Internet connection can be annoying. In other words, their performance to a certain extent is dependent on the efficiency of the Internet connection of the user. The browser performance also affects their efficiency. The reason for this is because data are loaded from a server where they are stored. Another disadvantage of this type of app is that developers don't have access to many APIs.

These apps also do not give the same advantage when it comes to distribution and monetization. For native and hybrid apps, they are made available in the app stores and this means that the developers will share in the ranking, feature placement and other marketing benefits of the app stores their apps are in. But each of these stores has its rules and regulations, which the developers must abide by in order to remain on the site. This is not the case with web apps, as there are no stores to put up the apps for sale in. Developers of these apps will have to depend solely on their marketing strategies and effort, as they will not get any marketing advantage.

Native and hybrid applications are monetized in the same manner. They can contain ads and in-app purchases, but the app store that provides space for marketing and selling takes commission for this service. Some app stores charge some amount of money before you can use the site or post your apps there. If you eventually make some sales, they will also take a certain percentage from what you have made. Monetization for web apps does not happen in this manner. Owners of such apps are able to monetize them through subscription fees and advertising.

Users of native and hybrid apps spend about 86% of their time using them, but for web-based apps, users devote only 14% of their time utilizing them. Native apps give a better user interface than hybrid and web-based apps.

I have taken time to explain the differences and pros and cons of these applications to enable you decide on which one to go into or which one will suit your requirements more. Knowing the pros and cons of each option, you can now on your own decide on which type of apps to go into at the right time.

Classification of apps based on functionality
Apps can be classified based on the purpose they serve. In this regard, there are as many apps as there are numbers of things that can be done

with computer-based devices including mobile phones. Here are various kinds of applications in this category.

Gaming apps

These apps are specifically designed to be of great help to gamers. According to researchers, up to 24% of all mobile applications are gaming apps. Some of these game apps are meant for children's use while some are for adults and grown ups. Examples of such apps are Candy Crush Saga, Clash of Clans, Angry Birds Go, Solitaire, Temple Run and many more.

Utility apps

As the name implies, these are the apps used in carrying out simple tasks useful to daily personal, household and office life. Though they do not have long session times, they are very much in demand. Users can use them as much as 4 to 5 times per week even though they spend fewer minutes on them. Developers of utility apps concentrate on increasing frequency of usage. Such apps include calculators, weather apps, communication apps and note-pads.

Entertainment apps

Entertainment apps are quite different from gaming apps regardless of the fact that each is meant to thrill its users. There are different kinds of these apps. In general, they are normal activities put into games with the aim of educating the users. Examples of entertainment apps are DubSmash, Duolingo, Ice Effex and Face Juggler.

News apps

News apps are highly relevant in the digital age of cyber journalism. Online media houses and new agencies make use of these apps to enable them to disseminate their news to their target audience quickly and also to make more money through ads. The apps generate money for their uses via sponsored content and native advertising.

Business apps/productivity apps

These apps are like utility apps, as they are basically designed to be used for the execution of various kinds of tasks such as shopping, billing, tracking of work progress, sending of emails, booking and many more. They make their users more productive. They are not the same thing as personal apps for reducing expenses and improving productivity. They also differ from B2B apps as well as office applications. Examples of such apps are Square Register, Point of Sale, Dragon Dictation, Facebook Pages Manager, Indeed Job Search, Voxer Walkie Talkie Messenger and Adobe Acrobat Reader.

Educational Apps

Educational apps are wide in scope. In fact, it is somewhat difficult to mention apps that should be listed under this category. This is because some apps may be educational to a considerable degree but in actual sense they do not perfectly fall into this category. But in general, apps that come under this classification are designed to give some lessons to their users. There are some suitable for students and schoolchildren as well as teachers and parents. Examples of educational apps are TED, Lumosity, Quizlet, Duolingo and Photomath.

Lifestyle apps

Lifestyle apps have wider coverage than any other type of apps because a lot of interests such as fashion, fitness, shopping, weight loss, diet, travel and others are covered. In other words, an app in this category can also belong to another category. They are made to help the users solve problems bothering their lifestyles. Thus, their applications make life much easier for their users. Under this category, we have dating apps, food & drink apps, travel apps, fitness apps, weight loss apps, music apps, etc. Examples of apps that can be classified here include but are not limited to The Game by Hot or Not, The DailyHoroscope, PINK Nation, AroundMe and others.

Travel Apps

As the name tells you, apps in this category are designed to ease the stress involved in travelling. With them, travelling will become more fun, comfortable, informative and much easier. There are some of them that can help a traveller to go to places he or she has not been before. There are some that will help you to plan your trip. Examples of travel apps are Google Earth, United Airlines, Airbnb, Fly Delta and Uber.

Social networking apps

Almost everybody makes use of this kind of app on a daily basis, as virtually everybody today uses one or more social media network such as Facebook, Instagram, Path, Circles, Twitter and others. Through these apps, you can easily connect with your friends and socialize with them.

Bear in mind that there are apps for everything. Why am I listing and explaining various kinds of apps? This is to enable you to know the apps to develop, their target audience and many more. With this knowledge, it will be easy for you to make a choice.

Now you know what apps are and their various types, it is now time to know what apps are not.

Difference between Apps, Programs and Software

Many people wrongly think that apps are the same thing as software and programs and thus they use the terms interchangeably, but the truth is that these terms do not mean the same thing in the computer and information technology industry. There are some differences, even though they are subtle. It is therefore pertinent to differentiate them so that you know their meaning when you are using them.

Apps as mentioned above are end-user programs. They cannot run on their own. They require an operating system to run. An app is useless if there is no system software it is meant to be used on. On the other hand, software is a set of data or program instruction read by a computer processor in order to execute an operation or a function. It is different from hardware, which is any tangible component of a computer. Software and hardware are not tangible, but a computer is almost useless without them. This is because without them all commands given to a computer will have to be typed. Programs dedicated to the management of computers can also be regarded as software. Typical examples of software include disk operating systems, file management utilities and others.

For the above, it can be asserted that an app is a type of software that helps the users to carry out certain specific functions. Differentiating between these two terms is like differentiating between rectangle and square. Software, like applications, is available in various kinds but not all of its kinds are apps. The same cannot be said of apps, as all are software.

In summary, software is a household name for any computer data but apps are specifically designed to aid the end user in carrying out a particular task. Apps can only be run on the operating system it is meant for. In other words, apart from hardware any other thing available in a computer is software.

Software is not necessarily an end-user program, but an app is.

Programs are also different to applications. It is a term used to refer to a set of commands instructing a computer on what to do. Not all programs are applications because they are not designed to serve a specific purpose for the end users. For example, every operating system has many programs running in the background, which are not meant for the end user. In contrast, all applications are programs but they are meant for the end users. For example, Firefore, Window Media Player and the likes have a graphical user interface and thus they are all applications.

Is Creating and Selling Apps Profitable?

I have spent time discussing apps, its types and how it differs from the other similar computer-related terms. Definitely, you may want to know how profitable it is to develop and sell apps as well as the cost implication of such a project. Though many people make apps for fun and some do it because they have passion for it, there is yet another group of app developers that engage in it as a challenge. But the truth is that the majority of app developers choose to go into the field for the gain their creations will yield for them.

Nowadays, a lot of people are going into app development and a huge number of people are learning programming with the intention of becoming app developers. The question is with the number of app developers in society, is it still profitable going into it, as it seems to involve doing the same all over again? If you want to go into app development, the growing number of app developers should be of no concern to you. This is because the demand for apps in the world today is high. As mentioned above, virtually all that is done with computers or online has its own app that helps the end user to achieve a specific target quickly and in a most effective and efficient manner. This shows you how large the app market is.

Based on industry reports, about 1.5 billion people worldwide are making use of mobile devices for one reason or the other. There is still another huge number that is using computers or computerized devices work. In hospitals and schools as well as other .ablishments, different kinds of apps are used to work. amber of app users throws light on the amazing , available for app developers in general and mobile app u~ ~n particular. Regardless of the number of apps available on various p~ .tforms, there are huge numbers of users to utilize them. For example, in the app store alone, there are up to 1.25 million apps available for download. With more than 50 billion downloads, developers of these apps have made up to $5 billion. Google, which is the largest Android developer, has 800,000 apps and they have paid out $900 million to developers for 48 billion downloads of these apps. These figures are quite astonishing. This tells you how lucrative app development can be. However, I have to warn you immediately. Not everybody that goes into app development succeeds. Some people end up in debt without making any profit from their efforts and investment. If you want to succeed in the industry, there are a lot of factors to take into consideration and there are certain things that you should do. First, your success in the industry depends largely on the pricing models that you are using (I am going to delve into this in detail in another chapter). Suffice it to mention that there are several monetization models such as, freemium apps, paid apps and paid apps with paid features. Other factors that will determine how profitable your app will be are the efficiency of your app, its usefulness, your marketing effort and strategy, and others. If you have a good app and you are able to aggressively market it to mobile app users, definitely, you will make enough money from it.

Common Concern of App Makers, Marketers and Sellers

First-time app developers do have some concerns, and sometimes these worries overwhelm them and discourage them from fulfilling their potential and bringing their ideas to reality. If you are just starting, bear in mind that you will have challenges but with determination and firmness of mind, you will overcome the fears. When you start having these worries, note that it is normal and that you are not the only person having them. At the budding stage of my career as an app developer, I got discouraged by a lot of worries, but I later continued thanks to some words of encouragement from a friend of mine. Here are some of the common concerns of newbies in app development.

App stores are filled with apps like mine

A good number of first-time developers are normally discouraged from making and selling their apps when they realize that there are apps similar to the one they want to make in the app stores, but this should not discourage you. Rather, it should make you be innovative and look for a way of adding more features and value to your creation. It is normally difficult to get an app that is the first of its kind on the market. So, when you discover that there are apps like yours in app stores, the first thing you should do is to check its ranking among other apps in the same category. Poor ranking tells you that the apps are not high in demand or that they have serious flaws, which make consumers not want them. You need to find out the cause of the low ranking.

If the apps have some downsides or imperfections that make consumers not want it, you have to take an innovative approach in creating yours. Take time to study these imperfections and then overcome them in your creation. Spend time at the planning stage to make sure all downsides are removed. You can only think of making money from any app if it is incredible in design and other aspects.

No money to begin the project

At times, you may have an idea and you are optimistic that if you finally put it into an app, consumers will crave for it. But you don't have money to create the app. App development is a costly project. This is why lack of funds is always a problem for developers, but there are ways to get started. You can start with the cheapest app builder online such as www.Buzztouch.com. It is also one of the most popular app markets. Build an app for the platform you have. For example, if you don't have a Smartphone but you have a PC, create an app for Android. There is no need purchasing a Smartphone. Start with what you have and when you have enough money you can try new things. However, it is difficult to avoid spending money. To publish an Android app with www.Buzztouch.com, you have to pay $25 for a developer's license, which will cost you about $99 if you are publishing an Apple app.

Can't share ideas in case it will be stolen

This is a common fear among beginners, and such worries a
reality. There are stories of people stealing other peop
taking glory and making wealth from what belongs
can only tell you to be prudent about it. Yes, th
another person stealing your idea when you

friend or a colleague can also help you to refine your idea and give you tips and advice that will help you to have a great app. In this regard, always listen and obey your conscience. If the inner voice in you tells not to share your ideas, I cannot advise you to disobey that voice. Secondly, know the type of person to share with. You should have a higher level of trust in a person before sharing your ideas with them. Besides, once you share an idea with a person, you should act fast in bringing it to reality. If the person is mischievous, you would have published your apps before he or she can think of stealing your idea or will be able to do anything about it.

Myths about App Development and Selling

The app development industry is one field that is so much in the limelight nowadays. A lot of things have been said about it, but not everything said about this field is correct. There is a lot of hype, misconceptions and myths about the industry. Some people have made costly mistakes because of what they hear about it. There are people with great app ideas but they are discouraged from acting on them because of the stories they hear about the app industry. On the other hand, there are people who enter into the field full of expectations and hope but along the line they become disappointed because they discover that the industry is not actually what they thought it to be. It is therefore important that you learn the truth about the app development industry. In this section, I am going to go through these misconceptions so that you know what the truth is.

Go for native apps

A lot of people belie͏   ͏ly way to enhance user experience is
throu͏   ͏ advise newbie to go into that rather
                            this chapter, I explained these types
                            es. Though native apps have some
                            ͏, it does not mean that one cannot
                            the section again to differentiate
                            ͏antages.

                            ͏ure of app development does not
                            ͏nder and CTO of Basecamp and
                            ͏ns why developing native apps
                            ͏nt. He highlighted some of the
                            ͏s that since users are no longer

e based on
e's ideas and
to other people. I
re is a possibility of
share with them, but a

interested in how an app is developed insofar as they are made in compliance with the store standard and that they are bug free, native apps may not serve the purpose that they did before. So, there is nothing wrong in giving other kinds of apps a trial and not limiting yourself to native apps alone. What is important is creating an app that is customer-oriented or useful to them. If consumers find your apps useful and interesting, they will definitely make downloads as soon as they discover the advantages it brings them.

You need to have a degree in computer science to create a hot selling app

Having a degree in computer science is only an added advantage. Without a degree in any computer science related field, you can still be a wonderful app developer. There are a lot of app builders that have no college or university degree. It is no longer news that Bill Gates had no college degree when he started his life as a developer. So, you don't have to abandon your idea or dream of becoming an app developer simply because you don't have a degree in computer science. It is sufficient for you to master your craft and develop the necessary skills to get started. In the labor market, employers look for people who are experienced and skillful in creating amazing apps rather than people with only college degrees.

You need to be an expert in coding and programming to get started

Indeed, app development requires at least some basic knowledge of coding and programming, but the truth is that if you have an idea, you don't need to be a skillful programmer in order to make it into an app and sell it. Nowadays, there are a number of freelancing sites where you can hire professional programmers. All you need to do is to hire a programmer that will put your idea into a functioning app. All you need is to identify bottlenecks in the market, provide solutions to them and look for a professional to enter into partnership with. Explain your idea to the person and make suggestions on how you will want it to be. However, it is important that you have a fundamental idea of the technology that matches your idea.

You will become a millionaire overnight with the sales of your app

If your intention of charting a career in the mobile app industry is to become a millionaire overnight, you may be dreaming. Many people enter into app development with such a mind set only to discover at last that it is not always like that. I have already spent time talking about how lucrative app development and selling can be but there are other things that are involved which I will explain later. Indeed, you can be rich and a multi-millionaire but there is no magic wand for achieving that. It is better you enter into the industry without having such expectations than to have high hopes only to be disappointed down the line. To make money from apps, it has to be great and attractive to the consumers. You also have to painstakingly market and popularize your app before you can make good money from it. App creation and marketing is an investment and requires patience.

It is cheap to develop an app

Though with the right platform, you will be able to easily develop an app, it is quite an expensive project. First, you will require money to be able to take care of all the expenses that you will incur like acquiring a developer's license and cost of publishing your apps in a marketplace or store. Marketing and promoting your apps, as we shall see later in this book, can be very costly and time-consuming. Besides the monetary aspect, it is an energy-consuming project. You may have to sit down for hours trying to promote your app. Some marketing strategies like the use of billboards are also capital intensive. Therefore, don't think that app development is a cheap deal. You may have access to a free tool to build an app but it does not end there. There are other things that will require money, time and effort.

Aesthetics is key

Another widespread myth about app development is that your app has to look aesthetically great before you can make money from it. Indeed, it is good that you have a captivating product. An attractive app is easily marketed. However, consumers prefer efficiency and content to visual appeal. In other words, if your apps are only visually great but do not have great performance and functionality, you may not have enough downloads. Consumers download only apps that are helpful to them or apps that will help them carry out certain tasks. Remember apps are end-user programs, so creating an app with grandiose presentation and fabulous design makes no sense if efficiency and effectiveness are not incorporated into it. A good app needs to be simple, efficient and attractive. It does not have to be attention-seeking apps only.

Aesthetics/presentation is of no consequence

On the other hand, some people believe that aesthetics or presentation plays no rule in the development and marketing of an app. I have explained above that your app needs to be efficient, effective and useful to consumers before it will sell, but I also mentioned that a good app is one that is simple, efficient and appealing. So, the aesthetics of your app matters a lot. It is not good to have an app that is just plain lacking in grandiose, color and design. The first thing that attracts a consumer is the look of your app, so make it is appealing to consumers so that they will think of downloading it. However, in your packaging, you should take into consideration the age that it is meant for. Everything in the package including the text font, graphics, color etc. should grab the attention of the target market. In a nutshell, a good app should be an embodiment of function and aesthetics, but don't over emphasize visual appeal to the detriment of efficiency.

You're done once you develop your app

The successful development of an app is just the beginning of the journey. If you develop an app, no matter how effective and efficient it is, you still have the responsibility of promoting it in the market. This is where the bulk of the task is, as a lot of things are involved (I shall go into various ways of marketing an app in a separate chapter). Suffice it to mention that if you are not an expert, you should hire another person to help you because your success depends on how many downloads you record. Many mobile app users will definitely purchase your apps if they become aware of it. After marketing, there is also the task of analyzing the performance of your app in the market. You don't need a professional analyst to help you in that regard. You can do that if you really know what to do. There is also the task of getting feedback from the consumers and improving your apps based on consumers' reviews and comments. Remarketing and sustenance of performance also present different challenges to you, so you can see that the task just begins after the development of the app.

You have to be on top of the competition immediately

Many newbies in the app development industry are desperate to be on top of the competition immediately. There is nothing wrong in aspiring higher and working harder, but you should bear in mind that getting on top requires patience and it is a journey of one step at a time. The industry itself is competitive; you need to first of all study the basics and the competition and then develop strategy that will enable you to climb up. It is not something that you can do just in a day. There is a lot that you have to learn and do in order to get to the highest rung of the ladder. So, if you enter the industry with high hope of becoming a leader in a day or within a small space of time, you may be in for a huge disappointment.

Every mobile user will download your app as soon as it is released to the public

It is good to have some expectations, but it is not good to have unreasonable and unrealistic hope. Definitely, your app will not be downloaded by everybody as soon as it is released, no matter how wonderful it is. Most consumers are comfortable with the apps they have, so it will also take time to convince them to purchase yours. You need to engage in aggressive marketing and promotion to get many people know that it exists. With effective marketing and appealing promos, they will gradually begin to download it.

Making an app for iOS and Android has the same requirements

I once believed that there was no difference in the creation of apps for these different operating systems. These operating systems belong to two different companies that are competing against each other. Most apps for these OSs are not compatible, so you need to be a native app developer if you want to make apps for various devices with different operating systems. However, there are some companies that give developers the freedom of making hybrid apps for both iOS and Android. So, don't buy into the myth that making an app for one OS is like making one for another operating system.

Hiring freelancers is always best

I do make an extra income by developing apps for clients I get via freelancing sites like upwork.com, freelancer.com and guru.com, but based on my experience with some clients, some developers in these sites charge low prices but mess up the work. A good number of them claim what they are not. They use their clients' project as a learning tool. However, there are professional freelancers that can develop wonderful apps. Some of them also charge low fares. So, you can get talented developers from these sites just as you can get bad ones. In other words, they are not the best and not the worst platforms to hire developers in case you want a freelancer to work for you. If you are using the platform, you have to be very careful so that you will not hire newcomers to the industry with little or no experience.

Simple apps go through a simple development process
It is not always true that simple apps do not have any complexity in their development. Indeed, an app may be simple from the user's point of view but very complex for a developer. This can happen for a number of reasons. It all depends on the app in question and the requirements of the client. As a freelancer, I have won a project in which the client required me to build an app with a button and a screen. When completed, the app indeed looked simple, but building it entailed a lot, as I had to include certain functions such as recording capability, possible GPS integration, an audio player, account registration and login and a backend with an API for the upload and download of records.

You should have basic design knowledge to build an app
This myth is similar to the myth that says you should be a programmer or have basic knowledge of programming and technology before you can develop your own app. Actually, even though your app should look attractive as explained above, you don't have to be an app designer in order to have an app that is great. All you need in this regard is to look for free and inexpensive app backgrounds, templates and icons in the Internet. You can find good ones within the price range of $50 to $100 on a site like App Design Vault. Alternatively, you can also hire a freelance designer either online or offline. There is nothing wrong in learning the basics but it is not necessary.

Your app is your brainchild and so you don't need expert advice
You can hear some guys say that one does not have to consult any expert when building an app because it is your work, your masterpiece. This is not correct. Though it is your brainchild, remember that it is said that two good heads are better than one. In the modern app development industry, data research, testing, analysis, consulting and deliberate

decision-making are ideals that are pursued like virtues. Doing these or consulting others does not make your work less original. Instead, such practices help you to refine your idea and to come out with a sound and flawless app. So, while you trust in your ideas, it is also good that you put trust in others.

There are other myths circulating on the Internet about app development and app marketing which I did not cover here because this book is limited in scope. Consequently, I will advise you to carry out thorough research to verify the authenticity of whatever information you find through the Internet. Anyone can post anything on the Internet, but with careful and thorough research, you will be able to find out the truth. Ensure that you are getting information from a reliable source. Join app developers' forums. Ask questions in the forum about anything you don't understand. Professionals in the forum will clear your doubts.

Chapter 2: App Development

The first chapter of this book deals with the fundamentals. If you read through it carefully, you would have gotten enough knowledge about apps and what you should know before entering into app development. In this chapter, I am going to discuss app development properly. The objective of this chapter is to help you bring your idea to reality and create a finished, functional app. The various stages in app development, starting from when you have the idea to the developmental level, are dealt with. The chapter also aims at helping you avoid certain common pitfall and mistakes that many newbies make at this early stage. Read it carefully to know where to start your journey.

I Have an Idea but Don't Know What to Do

There are a lot of people out there who are passionate about apps and they have great ideas but they don't know what to do, or where and how to start. Some of these people never act on these ideas. It is a grave injustice to yourself, family, friends and mankind in general to allow a useful idea to die inside you when there are multiple ways to bring it to reality. If you have an idea of an app, here are some tips to help you get started.

Make a note about your idea
Ideas for apps sometimes come by intuition that you can forget or that will become unclear with time if you don't write them down. So, the first thing to do is to write it down when it occurs to you so that you will not forget it. This will also help you to refer to it and think about it when you have time. You can also discuss it with friends or experts.

Think about your idea
Ideas are like raw materials for building; it has to be refined in order to be turned into a finished product. So, you need to refine your idea. The only way to refine your idea is to reflect on it to know exactly how it is to be used. When reflecting on your idea, there are some important questions to ask yourself, which include the following:

- What exactly is the product?
- Who is it suitable for?
- How will people use it?
- What are they going to use it for?
- What makes it unique or different from other similar apps in the market?
- Why should they download it and not others?

It is important that you ask these questions. This is because the answer to these questions will help you to establish the superiority of your ideas over other existing apps. Besides, they will help in guiding you throughout the remaining stages of app development. This stage marks the beginning of the planning stage in the development of an app, so you need provide an answer to these questions before moving further with your project.

The answer to the first question tells you the type of app you will be making. I have taken time to explain the various kinds of apps. So, if you have forgotten go back to the section to learn more about them. Are you making a native app, web app or hybrid app? The second question wants you to define your target audience. It is wrong to build an app before defining the target audience. The best practice is to define who the app is meant for from the first stage before you build it. This will help you to know exactly what features to include in it. The third and fourth question will define the purpose, usage and features that are to be included in the app. The fifth and sixth questions want you to be innovative in your approach. It challenges you to make your app unique and better than what is already available on the market. You need to give the consumers reasons to purchase your app and not those of your competitors. You know, before you will release your app, they are using some apps already.

There are important decisions you have to make based on the answer you obtain from these questions. Most importantly, they will help you to determine whether your app will be in high demand in the market or not. Thorough reflection on your idea will also help you to cut costs and save time when you are actually developing your product. It will also help to reduce flaws and imperfections that normally come with newer products.

Another important consideration to reflect on is the tools you will require to bring the idea to a finished product. These tools include manpower, skills, knowledge and funding. Are you the developer or are you going to hire someone else to do it for you? What are the financial implications? Do have the resources to execute the project? Are there ways of cutting costs on it? How do I promote and market the app? Which app store will I publish it in? These are important questions to ask at this stage before you continue.

It is also of crucial importance that you get a notebook where you will be writing down the answer to these questions. You don't have to rush over the stage because it is the planning stage. It determines how successful your campaign will be, so you have to do it very well.

Research

You have done the brainwork, but you need to find out if your answers tally with what is obtainable in practice. This calls for research into the app market using your answers as specimens. This stage helps to rid your answers of bias and bring them to the level of objectivity. You should make effort to avoid all prejudices when carrying out your research. Take a scientific approach to it.

The first thing you have to do is to collect data, which can be through questionnaires, opinion polls or surveys. If you have reflected on your idea very well as instructed above, you should know who your target audience is and where to find them. So, you should look for data where they are. For example, if the apps you are thinking of developing will be used by teenagers and young adults, the right place to distribute your questionnaires or carry out your survey are places that have a large number of your population. Universities, colleges and high schools (secondary schools) are good venues to find your target audience. You can also find them in dancing venues, beaches and social clubs. Another factor that will determine where you should carry out your survey is the purpose the app is meant to serve. For example, if you are developing an educational app meant for undergraduates, you will not get any reasonable and sound data from schools including high schools because your target audience are found more in the universities and colleges and polytechnics. The same thing applies when you are developing an app for business purposes, children, married people, a particular gender, etc.

Therefore, decide on a data collection method and then use it where your target audience is to be found.

Don't be afraid to meet highly placed individuals and visit large establishments and organizations if they are the right people to provide you with data. Many collect data from the wrong people or at the wrong places simply because they are afraid of going to the right people or visiting the right places. If the right target audiences are company managers or high government officials, find a way to meet them. You can schedule appointments with them and interview them.

Apart from surveys, questionnaires, opinion polls and other methods of collecting data directly from the field, you can also use other research methods such as library-based research. Today, the Internet is a veritable means of obtaining information quickly and in most cases free of charge. Social media networks such as Facebook, Twitter, Instagram and the likes will be of help to you in this regard. Create an account with these social media networks. Make the effort to get as many followers and friends as possible. Create groups and forums. Throw up your questions to your followers, friends and group members. It is also good to join online forums for app developers. Many members of reliable forums for developers have experience in the industry. So, if you ask your questions there, you are much more likely to get a more reliable answer from an expert point of view from them.

Using the Internet requires a high level of diligence and action. First, you should learn how to make a good post on these social media networks and forums so that more and more people will respond to them. Sometimes, people post comments and ask questions in forums and social media networks but they do not get much response from their friends and forum members because they are not able to frame their questions very well. It is also possible to get wrong answers from people because of the poor framing of your questions. Consequently, if you are going to use social media and online forums for data collection, you have to learn the best way to do that. I will not be discussing social media usage here, as it does not fall within the scope of the book.

This source of getting information will also require your time. You have to take time to read all the comments no matter how lengthy or short they are. Put them together. Write them down or you can also type them on word or any relevant app. Save your time by writing a point once. Ignore points repeated in the feedback once you have written it down. Ensure that all useful comments are noted down.

Apart from online forums and social media networks, you can also read articles written on similar apps already existing on the market. Check blogs of your would-be competitors and private blogs for articles that give information and statistics on the app market. If you carry out thorough research on the market, you will definitely find an article that will give you useful information. However, you should also be careful with your sources. It is easy to get wrong information through the Internet. There are a lot of articles with false information. A good means of obtaining correct information is to ensure that the sites you obtain your information from are reliable and useful. Government sites, blogs of professional bodies or reliable organizations and agencies are more reliable than personal and private blogs.

Review sites are also good sources of information, but you need to know apps that are similar to the one you want to create. Take time to read their reviews and feedback they receive from the consumers. From these reviews and consumer comments, you will be able to find out their imperfections, strong sides, how consumers would have preferred it to be, their download rate and overall general star rating. This will help you to know how to fashion yours and the necessary features to include.

Library-based research
Depending on the type of app that you want to develop, you can also carry out a library-based research. Check local libraries within your localities to see if they have useful sources on app developments. Pay more attention to magazines and newspapers on IT, apps and computers. You are likely to get useful information from there about your app.

The next thing to do is to analyze your data. Data collected are like raw materials to be used for creating a product. They will have no meaning if you don't analyze them. It is through data analysis that you will be able to find out whether your app will be required in the market or not. It will also help you to refine your idea to fit into the market. The data collected will tell you whether to continue with the project or not. App creation is similar to the production of various kinds of items. Just as analysis of data helps producers to understand the nature of the market where their products will be sold, it will also help app developers to have a clearer view of the app market. For example, they will find out if there are similar products already on the market, how these products are selling, their drawbacks, how consumers would have preferred the product to be, their download rates and the likes. Data analysis therefore is an important aspect of research that will help you to create a more realistic and useful product. When you analyze your data very well, you will be more focused and know exactly where you are heading for.

Write down the results of your analysis. The work is half done if your research and analysis are well done. The result of your research analysis will be your guide and reference point during the creation of your app. In fact, your app should reflect your result analysis. Whatever you are building should be in accordance with your research analysis, which is like your findings. It will also give you a tit-bit of how your app will be received in the market.

Know your competitors

I have mentioned in passing that you should know your competitors. Many newbies in app development want to go into a virgin area. There is nothing wrong with that, but that does not mean that you should not look for opportunities in the already existing market. Even if the market is already stuffed, you can still make a name for yourself insofar as you have something valuable to sell. There are benefits and drawbacks of having competitors. If you have competitors, the research aspect will not be difficult for you. People can give you information based on their experience with similar apps, so you will know already what the consumers want and features that are redundant to them. You will also be able to obtain statistical information easily online. It can also help you to be more innovative. Once you know the flaws of a similar product, you will simply find solutions to them in your app and then retain their good quality. It will also help you to know whether your app will be in demand or not. On the negative side, if you are not hard working, you will be swallowed up in the market by competition.

If you know your competitors, you can easily obtain information from their consumers. Consumers or users of a particular product are in a better position to tell you its pros and cons. From their feedback and comments, you will be able decipher what they want and what they don't want. You will also be able to do a thorough comparison of your competitors and their products. This comparison will help you to find out the advantages each has over the other. It will also help you to know the methods they are using to penetrate the market and sell their products. When you will be marketing and selling your product, this particular information will be of help to you, especially if you are still new in the market. With this information at hand when developing your app, you should be able to discover ways their strength and weak points will give you leverage in creating something unique, new and more helpful to the consumers. You will beat them in the market if you are able to overcome their imperfections and retain their good sides in your products.

Creating a master plan with your findings
Now that you have your findings ready at hand, you have to develop a blueprint of your apps before writing it. Before drawing the cyanotype of your product, it is of crucial importance that you first discuss your findings with experts to enable you have a refined and finished master plan that takes care of all aspects of the data analysis and results. As mentioned above, this has to be carried out with caution. You should be careful who you discuss your idea with so that it will not be used by another person. If you have no trust in anyone, you can skip this stage and move to another stage. Having a discussion with another person on your findings may not be necessarily if you are very efficient in carrying out data analysis. You can try corroborating your findings and analysis by juxtaposing it with similar research in the area.

If you are going to hire a developer for the task, you have to share your findings and analysis with him/her and ask him or her to make any reasonable input. I will talk more about hiring an app developer in another section. Suffice it to mention that it is good to get a reliable developer to bring your idea into a finished product. A good developer should be able to make sound input that will make your idea finer than before.

I Have An Idea but No Money to Start

In the preceding chapter I have provided tips to app developers that have an idea but don't know where to start or what to do in order to bring their idea to reality. In this section, I am going to talk to another group of app enthusiasts, namely, those that have an idea and know what to do but don't have the funds to finance the development of their app.

App development is a costly project. You need to have a large budget before you can go into it. Many app enthusiasts are not able to act on their ideas because of lack of funds. If you are in this class of app buffs, there are ways out. You don't need to give up on your dream of developing an app until after you have exhausted all options of raising funds for yourself. Here are various ways you can raise money for the development of your apps.

Personal savings

You can engage in what is known as bootstrapping, which is a means of financing a project without getting financial help from any other sources. You can raise money by saving some portion of your monthly income. You can also raise money by selling your investment or through your business. Once the idea occurs to you, first decide on when to start its actualization, let's say six months from the date you have the idea. You can save towards this date. Decide on the portion of your salary to save. Manage what is left by making do with only your basic needs. You may be able to raise the money depending on the amount you receive on a monthly basis. If your savings from your salary is not enough to raise the money, you can look for other means like borrowing from your friends and relatives, but borrow only the amount that you will be able to pay easily in the future.

Loans

The governments of many countries today provide financial assistance to promising entrepreneurs including app developers in collaboration with the banks in their respective countries. Besides, many financial institutions and lenders in many countries on their own give out loans to individuals with business ideas and projects that are likely to sell in the market when it is unveiled. Check the government financial assistance programs in your home country to see if there is any meant for app developers. You can apply for loans from the appropriate offices or agencies handling the programs. Alternatively, you can meet with your bank to see if they can finance your project or give you loans for the execution of the project. Definitely, if your app is something that will move the market, every bank would like to finance it or lend a loan to the initiator of such a program. There are also private financial institutions that provide individuals with loans for funding projects and businesses. If you are using this option, it is good that you discuss the terms with the institution willing to provide you with the financial assistance. Look for a friend, family member or a colleague with experience in negotiating contracts and projects that can help you to negotiate favorable terms.

Friends and family members

Rather than borrowing money from banks and other lenders, you can also seek financial assistance from friends and family members. There is no doubt that your family members, relatives and friends will want you to succeed and so if they have the money they can easily help you. Borrowing money from friends and relatives has an edge over borrowing from banks and other financial institutions. It is most likely that your family members will not charge you any interest or require you to make any down payments before they provide you with loans. Besides, you will not be under pressure to repay them. The dark side of this option is that you may not be able to get enough money from them unless you have wealthy friends and family members. Everybody is also struggling to meet with their personal needs just as you are struggling to meet yours.

Angel or see funding

Angel investors are individuals that provide funding for the actualization of a business idea or concept initiated by an individual or a business with the objective of partaking from the profit accruing from the idea or concept when it eventually materializes. Thus, the money they are providing can be considered as an investment, which they will begin to recoup as soon as the idea or concept begins to yield positive results. Angel investors are wealthy and can provide you with enough finance for the development of your app insofar as you are able to give them the reason to invest their money in the creation of your app.

Note that any of the means of raising funds to start a business can also be used to raise funds to create an app. Your chances of getting the required financial aid are dependent largely on your ability to convince and prove to your would-be lender that your app will sell or get many downloads. This is because every lender will want to get back their money and also make profit from it. So, they will not give any loan or finance any business if there is no prospect in it. Business ideas without great prospect are very risky to invest in.

The Cost Implications of App Development

The entire process of producing and marketing an app before it starts to generate money for the maker can be very expensive. It is one of the many discouraging factors for a newbie, but app development and creation should be seen as a business. Thus, just as money is of crucial importance for the establishment of any business, it is required to create and market apps. Consequently, before you initiate the process of bringing your idea to the level of reality, it is advisable that you first make budgets of the amount that the entire process will cost. This will help you to determine if you will be able to finance the project. If you are going to borrow or use other sources of getting funds as discussed above, you will know exactly the likely amount to request for.

The cost of developing an app depends on a number of factors, which you should take into consideration when deciding on the amount to spend on your app. Here are the factors to take into consideration when determining the actual amount it will take you to develop an app.

The service you will need

Whether you are a developer or you are going to hire a company to develop your app, you are going to require multiple services. App development has two major angles. Here are the two actors:

- The app designer whose responsibility it is to make the visual content that will be imbedded into the app.
- The app developer that handles the optimization of the product for the iPhone and Android devices' requirements.

If you are a developer and you cannot design an app, you are going to hire an expert app designer to create the visual content of your app for you. This means that you will be paying for the services. Similarly, if you are a designer and you cannot develop an app, you are going to hire an app developer to code your visual content for you. On the other hand, if you can neither create nor design an app, you will require these two services. It is also possible to find a developer that can also design.

Besides these two service providers, there are other people that may be involved in the creation of the project in one way or another, especially if the app is being developed for a business. These people include:

- Account manager who, in collaboration with the product manager, links the clients and the developers and designers of the app.
- The product manager who functions as the director by supervising the creation of the app.

How much time is required for the development of the app
Another factor that will determine how much it will cost you to develop an app is the length of time required to bring the app to a functional level. Some apps take longer to be developed because of their complex nature, while some apps do not take time to be created. It is even possible to start and finish an app in a day, but there are some apps that may take weeks or months to be completed depending on the proficiency of the developer and the features to be embedded in the app. Apps that take more days to be built are normally more expensive to design than apps that can be completed within a couple of days. So, if it will take longer to develop your app, it is advisable that you have a larger budget.

The features in the apps
The features in an app will determine not just how much you will need for the creation of an app and its complexity but also how much time that will be needed to complete the app. Besides, a professional developer does not just include features without evaluating them to determine whether they will be useful to consumers or how consumers will find them useful. The assessment will also take time. The developer will consider such factors before charging for their services.

The tools that will be used for the creation of the app
As you will learn later in this book, different kinds of tools are used to create apps, but some of the apps are more expensive than others because they are more sophisticated and come with better features. Thus, the tool that a developer will use to create an app will determine how much he/she is going to charge for the services. If you are building

the app for yourself, the tools that you will use to create your app also contribute to the total cost.

The type of app you are building

As I have explained above, apps are of different kinds because they are used for different purposes. It is the function an app is meant to serve that determines the features available in it, which in turn determines how much time the developer will spend in writing and coding it. All these will also determine how much you will be charged.

If you are hiring an app developer, the most veritable means of determining the amount it will cost you to develop an app is to obtain a quote from an expert app developer. They will discuss and analyze your requirements with you, provide sound input and then provide you with an accurate quote. Since quotes are issued free of charge by many app developers, it is advisable that you obtain up to three quotes from different app makers. You can now do a thorough comparison of the quote to find out which one is the most affordable. There are also apps that you can use to compare the quotes.

App Cost Calculator

A lot of tools have been created to make the development of other apps easier. An app cost calculator is one of such apps that help app developers to determine the amount it will cost them to develop an app. The calculation is near to 100% accurate. The app calculator does the calculation taking into consideration the following indices.

Factors such as UI style, type of platform, access controls, user profile types, app monetization (if you are going to be making money with it) and others are taken into consideration.

Platforms and Tools for Building Your Own App

With the upsurge in Information Technology and the wide use of computers and mobile devices in the doing of business and other economic activities, many platforms have been introduced by experts to help individual programmers, or small and medium businesses, that want to develop an app without much difficulty. Whether you want to develop a mobile app or a desktop application, there are some apps that you can use to achieve this. Some of these platforms can be accessed with just a little amount of money while it will cost you a lot of money to use some others. You will also find some that are available for free downloads. Some of these platforms and tools are user-friendly and can easily be used by people with little or no programming experience. Let's start our discussion here with the various mobile platforms and operating systems that you can build apps for and tools to create their apps.

Mobile platforms to develop apps for

Here are the popular kinds of mobile devices and tools to create apps.

Android

Android is a popular mobile operating system. There are a lot of android-based phones and tablets on the market today, meaning that many people are using these products. If you are able to create apps that are compatible with such a mobile device, your chances of getting a lot of downloads are very high. Mobile applications that are compatible with Android can be created with Java for Android. Its software development kit is available for free download online. The kit is not difficult to use. In case you are confused about how to use any of its features, you can watch the "how-to-do" videos of the apps provided by Android. The kit also comes with instructions and guidelines on how to use it to develop apps. Technical articles are also provided in case you are confused. Contained in the kits are developer tools, source code, samples and emulators for the testing of the app. However, after creating your app and you want to upload it on Google Play, which is Android's marketplace, you will be required to pay a $25 developer's registration fee.

BlackBerry

BlackBerry is another popular mobile brand with wide usage across the globe. There are a number of ways to create mobile applications compatible with the mobile devices using BlackBerry platforms. Through these platforms, you will also be able to build themes, mobile websites and widgets. BlackBerry's app store is known as App World. Apps are not uploaded there free of charge. They normally charge per 10 apps uploaded on App World. However, check if there are promotions available because the company from time to time provides developers with promos. In some of these promotions, the upload cost is removed or reduced.

Apple iOS

iPhone apps can be created via the iOS platform, which has impressive functionality and a large selection of tools. Guidelines and tips for creating apps via the platforms are also provided by Apple in its iOS developer center. However, usage of this platform and the upload of apps will cost about $99.

Windows

The Windows platform interface is one of the most user-friendly – if not the most user-friendly interface – among them all. Windows also provides guidelines to app developers. There is also documentation on what is acceptable and what is not accepted by Windows. So, if you take time to read through the documentation, you will not have any problem with the approval of your app. There is no fear of rejection insofar as you abide by the instructions given in the document.

Now that I have explained the various platforms and operating systems that you can develop apps for, it is time to explain the tools that you can use for the development of the apps.

Tools to Use for Building of Apps

Here are some tools that you can use to create mobile apps.

AppMakr

This tool can only be used to create apps that are compatible with Windows, Android and iOS operating systems. It is a web-based tool. The tool comes with a number of features which include but are not limited to location-aware GeoRSS, push notification, JavaScript capabilities and custom CSS. This tool allows users to create various approaches for their apps using their existing content and social networking feeds. You can access the basic features of the tool free of charge, however its advanced features are not available for free. You will be required to pay a fee of $79 to use them for a period of one month.

GENWI

Genwi is designed to help developers create and manage apps for different kinds of mobile devices including Android, HTML5, iPad and iPhone. It is a good option for developers that want to make apps with stunning graphics, videos, audio, photos and other interactive features. The tool comes with a feature that makes it possible for developers to edit their exiting mobile applications anytime they like. There are also a number of features that will help the owners to monetize them such as in-app subscriptions, coupons, adds and others. The first three months of usage does not attract any charge. After this period of free trial, subsequent usage attracts some charges depending on the features used.

Mippin

Mippin, which is a London-based platform, is unique thanks to its ease-of-use. With it, you will be able to develop apps for various operating systems like Windows, iOS and Android. The strong selling point of this app is the flexibility it allows users. When it is time to sell your apps, you can send your apps to Amazon, iTunes, Windows and Android stores for $999 per year.

MobBase

MobBase is a suitable app for developers that have interest in music and entertainment. With the apps, developers can utilize RSS feeds to update their fans on the latest events and band news. From the platform, you will be able to post tracks for music enthusiasts to listen to. With it, they will also be able to provide information about tickets for different kinds of shows and events. It will also give them directions to various shows. The cost for the usage of these services depends on the platform the app will operate on. For Android apps, you will need to pay a $20 activation fee, while apps for iOS will cost $250 in activation fees. Support services are provided free of charge. The hosting charge is between the ranges of $15 to $65 per month.

MyAppBuilder

If you are building a native app for iPhone and Android, this tool will be useful to you. You will require a monthly subscription fee of $29 to use it. It is very easy to use. Even people without any programming and technical background can create an app with the tool. The tool has a feature for uploading videos, books and apps to the app store.

Appery

Appery is a cloud-based tool for the development of apps for Windows Phone, iOs, Apache Cordova and Android operating systems. It does not require the user to install or download anything before they will be able to use it due to the fact that the user will operate on cloud. UI can be built with this app using its drag and drop features. It also comes with a visual editor. In case there is a need for you to store data, with this tool, you will be able to get connected to any REST API and use it in your app. The tool makes collaboration very easy, as you will be able to share the mobile application you are developing with other developers, customers, and business users in real time. There are a lot of other things that one can do with this app. However, to have access to a complete range all features of the tool, you will be required to pay $180 for a period of one month, but the basic features are available for free.

Mobile Roadie

This tool is meant to be used for the creation of apps that can operate on Android or iOS. It is compatible with all types of media. Twitter, RSS, Google and News keywords are automatically imported. Users of this tool are able to chat with each other via the auto-refreshing fan wall it comes with. After the creation of apps, developers can preview their apps and view exactly how it will appear on the consumers' devices. The app is strongly designed to ensure that users don't make any mistake as they submit their app. It is able to verify correctness and quality of the content to be processed. Users are able to get content directly from their website and transfer them to the app and also to move content from the app to their website or blog. Mobile Roadie is coded in agnostic language and this makes it possible for data to be pulled in a number of formats including HTML, CSV, PHP, JSON and XML. With this tool, it is also possible for you to personalize the appearance of your app, which you can apply to other platforms. To use the core plan of this tool, you have to pay $125 while the pro plan will cost you $667 a month.

TheAppBuilder

TheAppBuilder works in two ways. First, the tool can assist you in creating your app's structure and feed it with its initial content. The second way of using the tool is to utilize the training provided by the online toolkit. It features a dedicate AppLibrary, which makes it possible for developers to give users access to several apps that you can personalize as your own brand. With the Active Directory integration of the tool, you will be able to secure apps with passwords and username. Apps created and secured with this tool can be posted in app stores and users can access them using their login details. Users are also able to edit and update their apps as many times as it is necessary for them.

Publishing apps on various platforms can also be achieved with this tool just at the click of the mouse. The tool is compatible with Android, iPad and iPhone, and updates appear live just within a minute from the time the changes are made. There are different packages with different prices, which will be made available on request.

Other tools that can be used to create mobile apps for different operating systems include the following:

- Good Barber
- Appy Pie
- AppyMachine
- GameSalad
- MobiCart
- RunRev
- SwebApps
- ShoutEm
- BiznessApps

If you want to build apps to be used on desktops of different operating systems, there are some tools that will be of help to you. Here are tools to enable you create such apps:

- Haxe
- Electron
- NW.js
- 8th
- B4J
- Kivv
- Xojo
- Enyo
- WINDEVExpress

Each of these tools has its own pros and cons, so before you use any of them, it will be good that you first take time to read their reviews to know their pros and cons and this will help you to make a choice.

How to Build an App

If you join app development forums, you will definitely read posts and questions like these:

- How can I build an app from scratch?
- How do I become a programmer?
- What is the easiest way to learn how to program or code?
- How do I learn how to code?

These questions are common among newbies, especially those that have no programming knowledge. Due to the rate at which these questions are asked, many experts have also tried to provide answers to them based on their experience and skills. So, if you perform a good search on any of these questions, you are likely going to get impressive results. It is not uncommon to find conflicting guidelines and tips from different blogs and forum members. This is because of the reason already mentioned above. Everyone talks from their experience; here, I am also going to provide you with tips on how to create an app based on my own experience.

Get the basic requirements

If you are building the apps by yourself, the first point that I have to emphasize here is that it can be quite challenging creating an app for any operating system for the first time, as there are a lot of things that are involved. Your initial step apart from what has been discussed above should be making an effort to meet the pre-requisites, which are basically "knowing a database query language" such as SQL. This is due to the fact that many apps need a database except those that don't interact with any database, such as Flappy bird. Secondly, you will require a basic knowledge of Devops in case you are building a web app, as this will enable you to establish the development environment/server so that you will be able to release the app.

It is also of crucial importance that you deepen your knowledge of HTML, JavaScript and CSS if you are going to be a front-end web developer. Codepen and JSfiddle are the right places to learn about these programming languages. In case you only want to learn about JavaScript, the right platform to use is Node.js. It is the back-end development's platform of JavaScript. MongoDB is based on Javascript and thus you can also use it. Learning any of the programming languages mentioned below will also be good:

- Ruby
- Go
- Java
- Python
- PHP
- C# (can be used to develop game apps)
- Lua (good for the development of games apps).

The programming language you need to learn if you are developing native apps are as follows:

- Java for Android
- Swift/Objective-C for iOS.

As mentioned above, learning these languages is not a must for those that will want to use the services of a freelance programmer or a programming company. Secondly, even if you are planning to build your app by yourself, you only need to have an elementary knowledge of these languages.

Define your interest

It is always good to develop an app in the area that you have interest in. This is required not just by the developer but also the consumer of the app. If you have no interest in your app, you are like a wine producer that does not like wine. How can such a wine producer know whether or not his or her wine has a good taste? Here are some pertinent questions to ask yourself in order to identify your area of interest:

1. What apps are you passionate about?
2. Are there apps that you cannot enjoy?
3. What type of apps can you not avoid using?

The answer to these questions determines your area of interest. Building an app you are passionate about is a veritable means of turning the entire process into fun. The exercise is unlikely to become boring and this reduces the possibility of stopping halfway.

Sketching your app

If you carried out thorough research and analysis of data as described above, it will be easy for you to sketch your app. The ideas of what you want are now very clear in your head. You have done the necessary research and have concluded what you want and your market. So, it is now time to make a sketch of your app's UI's wireframe with pen and paper. Ask yourself necessary questions. For example, wherever you put a button, it should be for a purpose, meaning that you should ask yourself the purpose of each button you put. This is to be considered a draft and not a final version, so you can make changes when necessary. During this brainstorming stage, write down how the app will work and determine its various functionalities. When writing down the sketch, don't forget to make it as simply as possible. You may have a whole lot of ideas but it will be good that you don't stuff your app with features.

Plan the UI Flow of your app

Now that the idea of what your app will be is clearer to you, the next task before you is to establish a roadmap for the UI flow of your app, which is planning how the end user will be able to use your app from beginning to end. Create every step they have to follow and also take into consideration all situations they will encounter as they use the app. Capture all use-cases.

The flowchart should contain all the necessary actions the consumers should take in order to use the app. For example, it should contain guidelines on how the users should create their account, login into their accounts, how to recover their password in case they forget it, what will happen if they use a wrong password and how a user should use each interface or what they can do with each user interface. You can do all these with paper and pen. Again, remember to keep it simple and avoid making a massive diagram.

Designing the database

Now that you have properly done the sketch, it is time to design your database. Take a critical look at your sketch or plan in order to decide the kind of data you will keep. For example, if users of your apps are required to create an account, then you will have to establish a feature for tracking user ID, username, password, emails, the account creation data, the login time and dates of each user. In other words, it is the type of app that you are creating that will determine what data to keep. In order to map out the data relationship, I will suggest that you draw a diagram of an entity-relationship model.

When designing the data, take the features that you will be infusing into the app in future into consideration. Determine whether your app will be interacting with a server or with an API. Draw a sequence diagram if there will be any interaction in order to have an idea of how the process will be. After planning the back-end, the next thing to plan is the front-end.

UX wireframe
Check online, you will be able to find a lot of wire framing and mock-up tools that you can use in planning your UX/UI flow. Typical examples of such tools are Invisionapp, Wireframe.cc, Framebox, Mockflow and Gliffy.

Designing the UI
You may not go through this stage, but it is good that you design the UI if you care about the look of your app or front-end development. However, you will need to have basic knowledge of app design before you can do this. In case you are not an app designer, there are some UI elements that you can use to improve the look of your app. Some of these elements are available for free:

- UI Dock
- Graphicburger
- UI Cloud
- Spriters Resources (which are good for games)

Note that what is more important in app development is the building of the functions and features. The look is important but not as important as the functions, so don't pay too much attention to that.

Building the function yourself
If you are developing your app by yourself, one important factor that you should always bear in mind is that it is not always good to make use of an existing solution. Sometimes it is good that you build something that is unique. So, you should be able to know when to create a unique app and when to utilize an existing solution.

Be calm
Sometimes, beginners are overwhelmed by the enormous task to be accomplished and some may end up being confused and completely lost. When you feel that you are getting lost, the best line of action to take is to calm down. Don't panic. Take a deep breath to stabilize

yourself. Things will become easier as you progress and gain more experience to hone and perfect your programming skills.

Finding solutions

Examine the sketch and diagrams you have made in the previous steps. Are there functions that you cannot create by yourself or that you are finding difficult to create? If the answer is yes, it is a good idea that you make use of some existing solutions for many of such functions like authentication, networking/routing, real-time syncing and UI-related components. There are a lot of online sources where you will be able to find backend-related components, gems, packages, etc. However, be careful with the way you make use of other people's solutions. It is not advisable that you use them blindly. At this early stage, you should not engage in building complex apps or apps with complex functionalities. Thus, keep it simple so that you will not have any reason to make use of components written by other developers.

As I already mentioned, it is of crucial importance that you study your competitors' apps. One of the reasons why you should study their apps is to be able to determine the reason behind certain decisions they make. You can use GitHub for research.

Bringing Your Sketch to Reality

Now that you have completed the planning stage, it is now time to build the app. You should definitely be excited at this stage. Here are some tips to help get started.

Concentrate on the building of functions of the app. You have to build the functions one after the other. If you have not completed any function, don't start another. In other words, finish the front and back-end code of a function before starting with another one.

Always track your progress. Create a checklist that will help you to track your record. The best way to do this is to prepare a to-do-list.

First, write tests for your function

Before you start coding the functions of your app, it is advisable that you first write a test, as this will help you to avoid mistakes or reduce their occurrence to the barest minimum. By writing a test first, your apps will not have a lot of errors or bugs. However, if you are developing a game app, you don't have to write a test, but if you're creating a big app that you will edit in the future to include more features, it is important that you do the test in order to avoid releasing a buggy app which you will definitely rewrite when you start getting lots of negative comments from consumers.

There are tools that you can use for testing. Some of these tools include PHPUnit for PHP, Jasmine or Karma for JavaScript, PyTest for Python, xCTest for iOS development and many others.

Learning Git will be of help to you when you are developing your first app. Git is a version control system and a complete repository of history. The tool has a tracking function and will help you in a number of ways. For example, it can assist you in data recovery and help you to undo mistakes. It is also a good tool to use if you have any plan of joining force with a team of developers in the future. In case you encounter any problem when you're using Git, there are a lot of articles that will provide you with tips on how to handle some of the problems you will encounter with the tool. Check them online.

Make use of Google and other search engine

The Internet is a rich source of information. Sometimes, you will get confused with a process. Google is the best platform to quickly search for solution on that. So, learn how to make use of Google in obtaining information. In case you become confused down the line or your coding is no longer working and you don't know why, ask Google and you are likely going to find reliable and expert solution. If you try searching on Google and you do not find any reasonable answer to your question, you should post the question on stackOverflow. While posting your query on StackOverflow, don't forget to indicate that you have carried out thorough research on your question. You are likely going to receive an answer to your question.

Some people have complained that beginners always find it difficult to make use of stackOverflow especially when it comes to framing their questions. If you are finding it difficult to use this platform or you are in a situation where you don't understand your problem and you are not able to frame it, you should consider seeking help from an experienced programmer. Don't be ashamed of asking a professional to help you with some difficult questions. Doing so does not make you inferior. In life, people learn from other people who are better than they are. There are a number of platforms you can use to get help from experienced programmers. You can use Codementor, which offers video chat sessions with experts. However, these experts charge for their services and the rates differ starting from $15 per minute.

Don't be afraid of mistakes or feel discouraged when they occur

Virtually every programmer grows and deepens their experience by making some mistakes as they build their apps. The experienced programmers you are seeing today were once fumbling when they started. So, when you make mistakes and even fail the test you have written yourself, you don't have to be discouraged. They should be opportunities for you to learn and improve on your skills. Though it is good to create a professional looking app with stunning features, bear in mind that there is no such thing as a flawless app. Think of any app that you consider to be best of them all; it is buggy in some way, so don't think that yours will be an exception. This does not in any way imply that you should not aim high or make every effort to create a high standard app.

Note that it is possible for you to spend hours, days or weeks working on just a function and yet it does not work or you are having a problem making it work. Coding new features and functions is not always easy. This is why there is always a need for new programmers. In programming, it is ok to make attempts and fail multiple times. If you have such experiences, keep trying until you get it right. Remember you are still beginning with little or no experience, so you will find it difficult to execute a number of tasks, even tasks that appear to be very simple. If you finally succeed in building your first apps amidst difficulty and mistakes, you will definitely be happy and have a sense of great accomplishment.

Releasing your app

Now at this stage, you have finally succeeded in bringing your app idea to the level of reality. After testing and making corrections, everything is working fine as expected. What is left is reaping the fruit of your endeavors. You can only do this by launching it to the public or consumers so that you will use it to solve one problem or the other. There are different channels or avenues through which you can make your apps popular and distribute to app users on the market. I will tell you more about marketing a product in another chapter.

Common Mistakes about App Development
As I mentioned above, it is almost impossible to avoid mistakes or to have bug-free apps. However, it is possible to minimize the errors. There are some mistakes that beginners make which they can easily avoid if they have done their assignment very well. Here are some of the common mistakes among beginners in app development.

Creating a high energy consuming app
If you really want your app to sell, you should try to make it energy efficient. Nobody wants to use an app that will quickly drain the battery of their mobile devices. Everybody wants an app that will consume less power so that they will not have flat batteries when they are on the go. Unfortunately, many app developers, especially beginners, make this mistake. They don't give much attention to the energy consumption rate of their battery.

Not testing your app on various screens of different sizes
There are many kinds of mobile devices. Even mobile devices running on the same operating system or platform differ in their sizes and screen sizes. So, if you are creating an app, don't forget to test it on different screen sizes to see how it will function on them. Testing them on different screens is of crucial importance because your consumers are not using the same type of mobile devices with the same screen sizes. If your app is great in a particular screen size but very poor in another, consumers will have different experiences using them. Therefore, don't assume that all of your consumers are using larger screens, which may be the situation if you are creating a desktop app. If you are including images in your apps, design and size them so that they can run on mobile devices. This means that their sizes should be suitable for the screen of mobile devices. However, reducing their size does not mean that you should bring down their quality. Make sure that you don't stuff your apps with images. Your app will perform slowly if it has too many images in it. When you are designing images always bear in mind that desktop computers have larger hard drive space and more memory than mobile devices.

Not using asynchronous design

It is not always good to assume that a consumer will have high-speed Internet connection to make use of a function of your app if it is one that taps into the cloud. This assumption is most likely to be true if you are developing a desktop app or software but for a mobile app, it may not be true. You should use AsyncTask to forestall the possibility of the application hanging when you are making an API call or when you are using remote services. Most consumers don't know that there may be short hangs in an app when something is processing in the background. Asynchronous cause and threads carry out the background action and still allow the user to maintain interaction with the app.

Creating an app that is not optimized for low bandwidth

Many locations in various countries of the world have access to highbandwidth. Given this, many developers, especially beginners, concentrate in optimizing their apps for high bandwidth users to the total disregard of low bandwidth areas. Always create an app that can be used by people in areas with high and low bandwidth.

Using UI elements that operate better with a mouse and keyboard

Many developers keep dearly to standard development habits of optimizing their UIs for keyboard and mouse input. However, times have changed with the invention of mobile technology. With mobile development, users utilize their fingers and thumbs to key in data in their mobile apps. You should build a user interface with components that users can easily type in values with their thumbs and fingers. They should be able to move to the next element just by tapping with their fingers.

Ideally, you should develop larger and finger-friendly UIs. They should not experience any difficulties in finding the options on the menu and scrolling to use other functions. It is a common mistake among beginners to have many small items on their UI, which will be difficult for users to find or tap. To avoid this mistake, when developing your app, always bear in mind desktop computers differ from mobile devices in many aspects. Users of mobile devices don't access options in the menu with the mouse. They tap, scroll and tap again and again with their fingers. So, if you are designing a mobile app, make it easy for users to access items on the menu.

Making an app for a platform to look like an app for another platform

I have taken time to explain various operating systems and platforms. Apps for each operating system have their unique look, but many beginners forget this fact when they are developing apps. You can find an app for iOS that looks like the app for Android. You should always adhere to the standard input elements of the operating system you are developing apps for. In this way, it will be easy for your user to identify common elements of the app such as menu drop-down, button and many others.

Supporting older version of the OS your app is meant for

In app development, it is good practice to show the minimum version of the operating system your app is created for that you support. Ideally, it is good to write code that supports newer versions. It is not good to support outdated versions, as this can result in a buggy app. It can also increase the time you need for coding and testing each previous version. From experience, it is common to see beginners that develop apps that support older versions of the OS their app is meant to run on. Some also worsen the mistake by testing the app to make certain that it can operate on that system without any hiccups.

Developing an app before establishing a marketing plan

It is a mistake to develop an app before creating a marketing plan for it. I have highlighted the importance of researching the market, the competitor and determining the marketing strategies for the distribution of your app in some sections above. So, go back to these sections to know why it is important to create a marketing plan at the time you are planning for the development of the app. Many beginners make this mistake because they believe that as soon as they finish creating and posting their apps in app stores, consumers will start downloading them. App marketing is not an easy thing to do. Regardless of how efficient, effective and useful an app is, if it is not properly marketed, it will not sell. The marketing strategies are planned before the app is created to make the process easy and also to determine how successful the exercise will be.

Best Practices for Having a Successful App Development Project

If you want to create an app that will easily become popular among consumers, here are practices to abide by:

- Don't forget to study the bad apps: It is by studying a bad app that you will be able to understand the reason why it is considered a bad app or why developers fail to have something successful.

- Always make user's security a priority: Hackers normally target mobile app users because of their large numbers. Thus, users of mobile apps prefer those that are well secured and protected against these fraudsters. Thus, if you want your mobile app to be a success on the market, it is advisable that you make security your top priority.

- Use actual devices for testing rather than emulators: Don't take the testing of your apps lightly as instructed above. It will be good that you make use of actual devices rather than emulators, which is a great tool for debugging and app development. However, emulators are needed when it comes to a complete simulation of a working Android device. Thus, it is good that you invest in a quality device such as Amazon's Testing Platform and other automated cloud solutions.

- Make it simple: The key to a successful app is creating a simple app. You should focus more on increasing your output and reducing the time you spend on the creation of your app. Try to build and publish your app within the range of six to eight weeks. In this way, you will be able to test a lot of ideas and establish a portfolio for the apps. With this, you are likely to be more successful with your app creation project.

- Persistence: Don't easily give up when the project is becoming more challenging. Take your failings as an opportunity to learn something new.

- Look for a technical partner: It is said that two good heads are better than one. It is not always good to work alone without having another person to reason with or assess your work. So, if it is possible try to build a small team of people with the technical-know-how and technical-know-why in app creation.

- One after the other: There is no need to rush over a function in order to start another one. Make sure each one is done well before you move over to the other.

- Don't over think the initial process: If the idea of building an app for anything occurs to you, I will advise you to start working on it immediately. Don't waste too much time trying to make up your mind whether to give up or continue with the project. Don't be pessimistic about your idea. Having negative thoughts about your idea can stop you from continuing or carrying it out to the fullest.

Chapter 3: Planning and Initiating Your Market Campaign

If you started from the first page, I believe that at this point, you have learnt how to start a project of app creation and how you can eventually create an app. But the creation of the app does not end the story. It could be regarded as the beginning. You still need to continue getting it right until you start making money from your app. This chapter introduces this new aspect of your app development project, which is the marketing aspect. Here, you are going to learn how to plan and launch a marketing campaign. Keep reading to know how to plan and start a marketing process for the promotion of an app.

Define Your Objectives

The first factor to take into consideration when you are planning your marketing campaign for the popularization of your app is your marketing objective. When you want to market an app through any means, there is always some purpose that you will like to accomplish via the campaign. This is your marketing objectives. Your marketing objectives should have the following features:

- They should be specific.
- They should be measurable, meaning that you should be able to quantify the progression of your objectives in order to determine whether you are achieving them or not.
- They should be attainable according to the level of your experience.
- They should be realizable with the resources available to you.
- They should be time-bound, meaning that their result can be achieved within a particular timeframe.

If you develop a marketing objective that meets these requirements, you are good to move on to the next stage. As I progress in the discussion, you will realize why it is important that you define your marketing objectives before beginning your marketing campaign. Suffice it to mention that in the process of marketing your app, you will from time to time refer to it.

Know Your Target Audience

Every marketing campaign should have a target audience. Your target audience refers to the people that you will want to reach. It could be young people, the aged, adults, a particular gender, schoolchildren, students, people in a particular field, an educational institution to mention but a few. If you start marketing without determining who your target audience is, you are like a ball floating on the ocean without direction. I have already talked about the need to know your target audience in various chapters of this book, yet many topics demand that I discuss it in different perspective. Of course, you cannot develop an app or market it without knowing who they are meant for, as there are no apps that are suitable for everybody. Read this section in line with what has been said about it in any chapter where it is discussed. Here are tips to help you define your target audience.

Has anyone downloaded your app?
If people have already started downloading your app, knowing who these people are and why they downloaded your app will help you to define your target audience.

Take a look at your competitors
Find out who your competitors are targeting. They are also your target audience.

Do an analysis of your app
You need to evaluate your app taking note of all its features and the benefits of each of them. Who do you think will want to get such benefits? List them. They are your target audience.

Limit yourself to particular demographics
Find out who among app users that are likely to download your app. Take note of their age, gender, ethnic background, occupation, education level, marital or family status, gender, income level and similar factor.

Take note of the personal characteristics of your target
When defining your target audience, it is advisable that you take into consideration the personal characteristics of the potential users of your

products, which include their behavior, lifestyle, interest/hobbies, values, attitudes and personality. You need to find out how your product will fit into their general lifestyle and match with their personal life. Questions to consider here are: What platform does your target audience use more often to search for information? What features do they prefer most? How will your target use the product? The answer to these questions will determine the personal characteristics of your targeted audience.

Assessing your decision

If you apply the tips mentioned above, you should be able to determine your target audience, but you need to evaluate your decision to see if you are in order or if you are making any mistakes. Here are some important questions to ask yourself in order to help you assess your decision:

- Is the number of people that satisfies your requirements large enough?
- Will your product really give your target audience reasonable benefits?
- Are they going to find your target audience useful?
- Do I have a full understanding of what moves my target audience into taking the decision to use my app?
- How easily accessible are they?
- Can I easily deliver my message to them?

The answer to all these questions will tell you whether or not you have chosen the right target audience. If you have not planned a marketing campaign before, it is likely that you may be wondering how you can find answers to all these questions. As I will always advise, ask Google and you will get a reasonable answer. Look for articles and blogs that deal with your target audience. You should also join online forums of app developers. The members of the forum will be of help to you. Conduct a survey on your own and also look for results of a similar one conducted in the past. This way, you will be able to find answers to all these questions. Note that defining a target market can be quite challenging, especially to a beginner. So, if you are finding it difficult, you should not worry. It is normal to have such difficulties.

Never Neglect Your Competitors

When planning your marketing campaign, it is of crucial importance that you know your competitors very well. They are already in the market and so have more experience and an edge over you as a newcomer. There are a number of benefits you will get if you take time to study your competitors and include them in your marketing plan. Here are the advantages of knowing who your competitors are:

- If you know who your competitors are, you will know their mistakes and learn from them.
- Knowing your competitors will help you to determine who your target market is and ways of reaching them easily.
- It will also help you to know which marketing strategies are effective and which ones are not.

In light of the above, when planning your marketing strategies, it is important that you make an effort to study the market in order to find out who your competitors are.

Who Are Your Competitors?

There is no business that has no competitors. In fact, the doing of business is a struggle in which only the fittest survive. This competition can come in many ways. It can be an existing or new app. It can also be a new field or approach that will make your own field useless. In other words, when researching your competition, don't limit yourself to already existing apps but also think of a possible new app in the same category as yours. You can find out who your competitors are from the following:

- Press reports
- Adverts
- Local business directories
- Consumers' feedback
- Questionnaires and survey
- Existing apps that have similar functions and features with yours
- The internet (search engines)
- Exhibitions and trade fairs.

If you are able to find out who your competitors are, there are some pieces of important information that you should know about them and they include the following:

- Their products
- The features and uses of their apps
- The number of downloads they have recorded so far
- The amount at which they are selling their apps
- Their brand and design
- The owners
- Their target audience
- Their locations
- The marketing activities and the medium they are using for marketing
- How they relate with their customers
- Their financial capacity.

With this data, you will be able to tell how intense the competition will be.

Ways of learning about your competitors
You can obtain information about your competitors using different means. Here are various means through which you will be able to get all the necessary information about your competitors.

- The Internet
- Exhibitions and trade fairs
- Directories
- Corporate registry (if they are within your locality)
- Yellow Book
- Consumers
- Direct interviews with your competitor.

When you obtain information about your competitors, it is of crucial importance that you evaluate it to find out whether there are prospects in the field, the strength of your competitors, their weak points, their marketing strategies, their customers, etc. It is not difficult to analyze your competitors based on the data you have gathered. List all you have gathered about them, categorizing them into three. The first category should be titled what you can learn from them and what you can do better, what they are not doing fine and what they are doing in the same manner with you. See ways to improve on what they are not doing fine or even what they are doing in the same way with you. Make sure that your potential users will have a reason to purchase from you and not their previous customers.

Determining the Best Channel to Get Your Target Audience

Your marketing plan must stipulate your marketing channels, which are the various ways through which you can reach your target audience. They are classified into two broad categories, namely, direct and indirect marketing channels. In the former, the consumers get your products directly from you and in the latter, they get it from secondary sources. In the app industry, many developers market and sell their app via the Internet. There are a lot of marketing channels (some of which are direct and some are indirect) that can be used to reach a target audience in app development marketing. Examples of online marketing channels are social media, display ads, blogs, print ads, affiliate marketing, app store, e-commerce website, online marketplace like Amazon, newsletters, contests and many others. I am going to discuss some of these channels in the next chapter, but the question is how do you determine the best marketing channels to reach your target audience?

This is not an easy question to answer, as all online marketing channels on the Internet are efficient insofar as they are well utilized. Besides, most of them are connected and can be used simultaneously. For example, you can promote your apps in a blog and through social media platforms and link them to your website or the app store where your product is made available for download. It is possible for a developer to market directly and indirectly to consumers. For example, Apple market their apps directly to their users and also sell indirectly through a number of partners. They also make revenue by selling other developer's app.

However, it is your target audience and your app that determine to a greater extent the right strategy to use. The basic question to ask yourself is which platform does your target audience visit most often? Again, I will suggest that you look at your competitors. You can take a cue from them. The first factor to take into consideration when deciding the best marketing channel to use is whether you want to sell directly or indirectly to your users. Most beginners sell indirectly as they don't have money to build an ecommerce website where they can sell directly to their consumers. But if you have no ecommerce, you will be an indirect seller, meaning that you will be partnering with a business that has an ecommerce site. For example, there are a lot of developers selling their apps in App stores, Amazon, Sears.com, Esty.com, Buy.com and other marketing places. If you are going to sell direct, it will be good that you have a reliable website with all the necessary features. If you are choosing other marketing channels, make sure that you go for one that is highly reliable and popularly known for app. The best option should be to use multiple options.

When you have decided how to sell your app, you can now align it to your marketing channels, which can also be direct or indirect. Direct marketers normally concentrate on a particular message for their app to their users. Various ways of achieving this are known as direct marketing channels. They include email marketing, print ads, display banner ads, search ads, remarketing and affiliate networks. Indirect marketing channels on the other hand refer to various ways of creating awareness about your app. They include social media, network ads, thought leadership (making contributions on authoritative and industry related websites), blogging and press coverage.

There are some factors to take into consideration before choosing a marketing strategy. These factors included the following:

- Available resources to use a platform
- The conversion of a channel
- Sales and profits
- The available manpower
- Cost, benefits and disadvantage

A thorough consideration of these factors will help you to determine the channel that is most suitable for you. When you have considered these factors, before making a choice, list all the marketing channels that you are considering in the order of their preference and according to what will give you the most benefits. This list will help you to choose the best channels to use together.

Marketing Mistakes to Avoid

When you are planning your marketing campaign, there are certain mistakes that a good number of beginners make that you should avoid if you want to have a successful marketing campaign. Here are some of these pitfalls to be aware of.

Failing to consider your app's customer base

When planning your marketing strategy as instructed above, it is of crucial importance that you think of your customer and a way of getting feedback or communicating with them. Any consumer that downloads and uses your app is in a way having and using a part of your business. Thus, you should seize that opportunity to communicate with the person. Consumers feel appreciated and belonging when their opinion about the performance of the product they are using is sought for. Thus, when planning your marketing channels, don't make it a one-way traffic that only you can use. If you talk them into purchasing your product, you should also give them the opportunity to talk to you and tell you what they feel about your product and whether or not they have any regret purchasing it. So, establish a platform for review. It is a costly mistake to deny consumers that freedom to provide feedback on the product they have been using.

Buying into the myth of app store optimization

Just as search engine optimization helps websites and blogs to remain visible on the search engine, app store optimization makes apps well ranked and occupy a prominent position in the app stores. However, a lot of myths are circulating on the Internet about app store optimization. It is important that you are aware of these myths and avoid them. Here are some of the most common ones.

1. Changing app titles regularly to improve ranking
There is the myth that one can improve their app store ranking and adjust to trend by changing titles of their apps. The title is a very important aspect of app store optimization, but changing the title of your app regularly will not be of any help to you. Instead, it reduces your ranking. This is because changing your titles means that you are starting afresh. The implication of this is that your previous ranking will

drop. In other words, think twice before you choose your title, as it will remain throughout the lifespan of your app.

2. Keywords are insignificant

Many app marketers, especially newbies in the field, think that keywords don't have significance in ASO (app store optimization). They hold onto this belief because of the conception that SEO and ASO don't have the same rules and guidelines since they are completely different strategies for different things. The truth is that despite the fact that they are not same, they have certain similarities in terms of rules guiding their usage. For example, in both strategies, it is of crucial importance that you take time to research your keywords and avoid stuffing contents with them.

3. Reviews are the most important

Some people believe that their apps will sell once they have good reviews. With their ratings, people will easily download their apps. Indeed, positive reviews speak well of the developer or the business that owns the app, but they are not very important when it comes to getting people to download your app. This is because they don't help your app in app store optimizations. Ratings help consumers to feel appreciated and to contribute to the growth of the business they rated.

4. Making unrealizable promises in your commercial

One of the biggest marketing mistakes that many developers, especially newbies, make is to oversell their apps. Many people do this because they believe that their apps are of great quality and that consumers will like them when they begin to use it. It is not good to make promises and claims in your ads especially if these promises and claims are not realizable. Don't think that your target audiences are morons with little or no memory to remember things. When the users of your apps discover that all your claims about your apps are not actually what are obtainable, they will definitely leave poor feedback for you and discourage others from buying. You know already what will become of your app when this happens.

5. Not popularizing your apps via a number of platforms

Your app's download rate and the profit you will make from it will be determined to a greater extent by its popularity among consumers. If you don't engage in aggressive marketing using different platforms and means, many app users will not know more about your apps. So, don't make the mistake of promoting your app only in a platform. Use many of them such as Facebook, blogging, Twitter, App Store Optimization, Search Engine Optimization (for your blog and website), Instagram and others. You can reach millions of people through each of these platforms and marketing channels.

Chapter 4: Promoting and Popularizing Your Apps: Ways

Now that you have learnt how to plan and initiate an app marketing strategy, the next thing to be done is to go into action. Start marketing your app using different means as instructed above. In this chapter, I am going to tell you the various ways of promoting and making your apps very popular among app consumers. You may not be using all. But as I advised above, it is a mistake to use only one as it limits the number of people that will be aware of your app. Here are the popularly used means of marketing apps.

Don't Overlook the Power of App Store Optimization

App store optimization, which is normally abbreviated as ASO, refers to the act and process of making a mobile app more visible and increasing its ranking in an app store such as Google Play, Window Store, iTunes and BlackBerry World. Normally, consumers pay more attention to apps that are highly ranked or that are occupying prominent positions in app stores than those that are ranked on the last pages. Many app users don't have the patience to scroll down when they are searching for apps in these app stores; they restrict themselves to those on the top. You can see why it is important that you invest in app store optimization.

App store optimization also encompasses what is known as the conversion rate optimization (CRO), which refers to all the activities carried out in order to improve the rate at which the app store impressions are converted into downloads. It is a common belief and experience of marketers that highly ranked apps have a higher conversion rate than apps with low ranking.

Why you should include app store optimization in your marketing strategies

When it comes to app marketing, app store optimization should be regarded as an important and irreplaceable strategy. Apps featuring on the top chart are not there by chance. The same can be said of great downloads. If you really want many app consumers to see and download your app, you have to invest in app store optimization. With the process and activities, users on the app stores will find your app easily when they are searching for apps. According to statistics, 65% of app downloads are carried from App Store searches.

Another reason why you should invest in app store optimization is that it is a veritable means of taking your app to the highest level with your competitors being ranked below you. If you are ranked higher than your competitors, you are more likely going to get more downloads than them because of the reasons mentioned above.

App store optimization is also a good means of ensuring that you are ranked higher for a particular keyword in the app store. When users search for such a keyword, you appear first before your competitors. This will also help you to get more downloads than your competitors.

ASO also helps you to optimize app store assets such as description, promo video, icon, screenshots and others. The optimization of these assets enhances download conversion rate from keyword searches, top chart impression, store features, etc.

Two Ways of Optimizing Your App in An App Store

There are basic two methods of app store optimization used by many ASO marketers: conversion rate optimization and keyword optimization. In the latter, the ASO marketer aims at higher app ranking by optimizing the keywords in the metadata of an app. The algorithms of app store keywords will identify the keywords when consumers are performing searches on it and then rank it very high in the search engine results page. The ASO marketers using this method infuse the right keywords into the metadata of the app. In the first method, ASO marketers optimize app's assets in order to increase their apps' downloads. I will examine keyword optimization in detail here.

Keyword Optimization

Keywords are very important, as they can affect the ranking of your apps in the app store. A keyword is basically the crux of what your app will do, for example "photo" if the app is photography based. It is important that you include the keyword in your app title even though some people may not consider this practice as very crucial. A report by MobileDeveHQ shows that app marketers that include their keywords in their title get about a 10.3 percent increase in rankings.

However, experts do not agree on the importance of the inclusion of keywords on app descriptions. Some are of the opinion that including keywords in the title plays little or no role in the ranking of apps because they are not searchable and indexed for ranking. But there are some experts that are of the opinion that descriptions should have the keywords. In the midst of these controversies, I will advise you to add it in the description of your app, especially in the introductory aspect of it, considering the fact that your description makes your apps sellable to the users.

How to find keywords for apps

If you know how to obtain keywords for search engine optimization, you will be able to find keywords for app store optimization because the processes are almost the same. Your keywords and phrases should have the following qualities:
- They should have high volume of searches.
- Their relevancy should be high.
- Good keywords and phrases are not highly competitive.

There are some tools you can use to search for keywords for app store optimization that have these three qualities. A typical example of such a tool is the keywordTool.io. I will advise you to first look for relevant keywords in this tool or any other one before you give your app a name. This will help you to find a suitable name for your app, which you will not have any need to change in the future. I have already talked about the implication of changing an app's name. You can see why it is good to first research your keywords before naming your app.

Kinds of searches to be optimized

When researching your keywords, it is important that you take into consideration the kinds of searches in app stores that are very common among app users.

1. Genre searches

Many app users search for apps on app stores based on particular categories such as business, games, accounting, etc. So, when you are searching for keywords to optimize, it is advisable that you consider the genre to optimize with the keyword. It is best to go into a less competitive genre. In order to optimize an uncompetitive genre, you need to discover the trend on time before it becomes competitive. Optimizing the right genre with the right keywords is very important. This is because up to 80% of all app store searches are for particular genres.

2. Inspirational searches

Between 5 and 10 percent of users get involved in inspiration searches, which are mainly meant for subjective keyword phrases such as new games, best to do list and others. It is important that you make use of inspirational keywords in your ASO strategy. The problem with inspiration searches is that it is not always easy to include them in your app title. If you cannot include them in your title, make sure that they appear in the description of the app. 5-10 percent of app users search for subjective keyword phrases.

3. App titles

As already mentioned, you need to incorporate your keywords into titles to improve your ranking rather than depending on brand recognition. This is because app store searches that are specific app titles constitute only 5% (or even less) of the total searches in the app store.

4. Transactional searches

Each app performs specific functions and some app users search for apps based on their functions. However, only 5% of users based their searches on the specific function of their app. This explains why it is necessary that you incorporate the specific tasks your app is meant to perform in your keyword. If it is possible, include them in your app name, but this can be very difficult to achieve. Examples of phrases and words that indicate functions and tasks are "organize tasks", "resize image", "send emails", "make payment", etc.

Localized Keyword

A good number of app marketers, especially those still new in the industry, don't know the importance of the localization of keywords. Keywords localization is a process of utilizing different languages for your app mane, screenshots, keywords and the likes. The process can be very taxing but it is also beneficial, as it can multiply the amount of downloads you will receive. It is not difficult to use localized keywords. Google Play comes with a number of features that make localization very simple. For example, there is a feature that will automatically translate from primary language to other languages chosen. If you are an Android developer, go through the localization checklist of Google for proper guidance.

Understanding the Role of Downloads for ASO

Though you have no control over the download you are expecting to get after engaging in a successful marketing campaign, there is still a need for you to have a proper understanding of what downloads do in app store optimization. Your ranking in the app store search is dependent to a considerable extent on the number of downloads you have. Put differently, the app store search algorithm also considers your downloads for indexing and ranking. If you have many downloads, you are much likely going to be well ranked in app store search engines but if you have fewer downloads, your ranking will be affected. You need to make sure that you have a high number of downloads so that you are on the top of search results. To achieve this, you should ensure that many people know about your apps. The more they know about your app, the more they are likely to download your apps and the more your app is likely to be downloaded by other users. You can see that this is a continuous process. It is not something that you will do now and stop doing it in the future. The result you will obtain is also cumulative, meaning all aspects are important. If you don't get any of them right, your success will be affected.

The Effects of Rating and Reviews for App Marketers

Your rating and reviews determine to a great extent how your prospective users will assess you before downloading your app. You have no control over these reviews and you cannot add or delete them. Once they are given, there is nothing that you can do in order to improve them or reduce their impact. It is therefore good that you ensure that you get a positive review starting from the beginning. Many people request their users to leave positive feedback for them. You may consider doing so, even though it is not the best practice or the best approach. There are tools that you can use to solicit positive reviews from satisfied clients. This will also help puncture negative feedback.

Icons and screenshots optimization

When optimizing your app, don't forget your screenshots and icons. They represent your apps and brand virtually. You should make them very attractive so that users' attention will be attracted by them. Once their attention is captivated, they will want to know more about the app and how it will benefit them. Test your images through Facebook Fb+1.23% before releasing your app.

Optimize your website for app-related searches

It is good that you have a website or blog of your own which you have to also optimize for app related searches. Many Internet users first perform Google searches on their favorite apps before looking for them in app stores. Some also come to Google to search for articles and reviews of the apps that they are interested in before searching for them in app stores. This explains why app related searches are progressively becoming popular starting from 2009. This is evident from Google Trends data for apps.

ASO Best Tips and Practices

Here are some ASO tips that you can apply.

Have deep knowledge about your target audience and competition

I have already highlighted this point in a chapter above. If you are to make use of ASO, it is of crucial importance that you know your customers and your competitors very well. The best way to know your customers is to put yourself in their shoes. In your search for the right keyword, ask yourself what type of searches the consumers will actually be doing in order to arrive at your app and the normal phrases they are likely to use in their searches. The answer to these questions will help you to find relevant keywords. Apart from studying your customers, you should also carry out thorough research on your competitors. This will help you to find out the keywords that are normally targeted by developers that have similar apps with you.

Get the right name for your app

A good app name as mentioned above should contain relevant keywords, as it enhances app store search results.

Make full use of your keywords

Whether you are optimizing in the App Store or Google Play, make full use of your keywords. The keyword field of App Store can only accommodate 100 characters, which includes the title. Therefore, ensure that you exhaust the 100 characters. In Google Play, developers are allowed to describe their app in 400 characters. While describing your app, ensure that you use as many relevant keywords that can naturally fit into your sentences.

Write a compelling description

Your app description should be written with the relevant keywords in such a manner that they talk to the reader about your app. You should concentrate on making your prospective clients download your app. So, ensure that you use some call to action words and don't focus on search engine index. Adjust your description if you submit an update so that it will reflect the changes.

Include screenshots and videos

Screenshots, videos and icons generally will not make you more visible on the search engines but they will help in increasing downloads, which also improve visibility on app stores as mentioned above. With the images, your consumers will be able to have a mental picture of what your app is all about even before using it.

Use promotion to drive traffic to your listing

Google and Apple normally consider backlinks to pages and amount of traffic coming to an app and product page when ranking it. This highlights the fact that you need to make use of other means in increasing traffic to your app page. I shall discuss some of these means in the subsequent sections, but suffice it to mention that apart from on-page optimization, you have to engage in other kinds of promotion in order to drive more traffic to your app page.

Keep your app up to date regularly

Regularly gather customer feedback and improve your app based on that. Make sure that you improve on what you have before. This will make users rate you highly. App stores also value apps that are frequently updated to be abreast with new findings in the field and to meet consumers' expectation. If you update your app, make sure that you get consumers to download the update.

The application of these tips and guidelines will help you to have a well-optimized app, which will be highly ranked in the app search engine.

Take Advantage of the Social Media Networks

Today, social media marketing is widely used by many app developers and businesses to promote and popularize their apps because of their efficiency in increasing brand and product awareness. Each of the social media networks such as Twitter, Facebook, Instagram, Pinterest and others have millions of users. Millions of these users visit their pages on daily basis. Thus, if you are able to apply the best social media strategies, within a small space of time, many people will be aware of your app. Definitely, if they are impressed with your commercials, they will begin to download your app. In the subheadings below, I will provide you with tips on how to market an app on some of the popular social media platforms. I will come to how to use a website to promote an app but suffice it to mention that you should have a website for promoting your app. Always include links to your app at the end of each post or article in your website.

Popularizing your app with Facebook advertising

Facebook advertising is an effective means of marketing your apps and generating app installs. Here are tips to help you get started with Facebook marketing.

Determine your target audience

Facebook is the most popular social media network today. It has millions of users, but not all these users are interested in your apps. It is a waste of time and resources to market your app to a person that has no interest in it, so it is advisable that you define your audience and target it. Use the following tips to define your audience:

- Demographics
- Location
- Interests
- Advanced targeting
- Behaviour.

Show the benefits of the features of your app

In your Facebook ad campaign, ensure that you highlight the benefits of your app. This means that you should tell your audience more of the reasons why they should download your app rather than telling them what the app is.

Create a Facebook page and optimize it for SEO and Likes

Creating a Facebook page is a stepping-stone to anything you want to do on the platform, but it is also important for app users to easily find you on Facebook and in Google when they perform searches on your app. You can achieve that by optimizing your Facebook page:

- Choose a descriptive but easy-to-remember username (your username can be regarded as your URL).
- Talk about your app in the *about* section using descriptive keywords.
- Make sure that you classify your business in the right category.
- Optimize the images on your page, especially your cover and profile photos.
- Pin a post on the top of your page and make people like it (by liking the pinned post, they will continue to get your posts in their newsfeed).
- Create a Facebook Group for your target audience (this group provides you with the opportunity to interact with your target audience).
- Use Facebook Buttons and Plugins to encourage social sharing.
- Try having a large number of friends and post regularly about your app to reach them.

Posting at the right time

It is not enough to post on Facebook as a means of promoting your app. You have to ensure that you post at the right time and keep to the right posting frequency. Regarding the best days to post on Facebook, there is no generally-accepted day to post but some studies have shown that it is more effective when posts are made on Thursdays and Fridays. Many experts suggest posting between 1pm and 3pm. The posting frequency should be around 5-10 posts per week.

Extend the reach of your posts by boosting them

When you create a new post, look for the boost button and click on it. The feature is also available on old posts. It helps you to determine who you want to share your post with. You can share with all your fans on your fan page or with a particular set of people through the targeting option.

Facebook app marketing don'ts
Here are some Facebook marketing don'ts to be aware of:
- Don't use an unrecognizable profile picture
- Don't have an empty *about* page
- Don't violate the terms and conditions of Facebook by using a dummy account
- Don't bore your fans with too many posts
- Don't disregard multimedia posts
- Don't fail to give quick responses to comments
- Avoid making assumptions.

Get Active on Twitter
Twitter is another popular social media network that you can utilize in promoting your apps among app users. As of November 2013, there were over 232 million active users of this platform, so you can see why many businesses are promoting their products on Twitter. You too can promote your app using this social media network. However, you need to know the nitty-gritty of marketing on the site. Here are some tips that you can use to promote your app on Twitter.

Create a compelling bio and optimize it
Create a bio that tells your followers who you are and what you are into. It is a wonderful idea that you include a link to the landing page or website of your business. Be consistent in the manner you speak so that people will understand who you are and what you are into in clear and simple terms.

Discover experts and influencers in your niche
Search keywords that relate to your niche on Twitter search or tools like Topsy in order to find out who the influencers/media, customers and people with similar ideas like yours are. Establish a relationship with them by following and interacting with them every day. You can create a list of popular bloggers, writers, journalists, potential partners, possible customers, big businesses and include them in a private Twitter for the purposes of interacting with them on a regular basis. Focus on establishing a relationship and synergy rather than promoting your app.

Tweet often

It is a good marketing strategy to be tweeting regularly on Twitter. If you really want to promote your app via Twitter, you should make effort to tweet once a day. In this way, you will maintain interaction with your audience on a regular basis.

Allow followers to share content

A good Twitter marketing strategy is to encourage followers to re-tweet your tweets. Don't be ashamed to ask them to favorite or mention your tweet insofar as they contain useful information.

Know what is said about your app

You have to keep track of the app in order to know what your followers are saying about your brand. If there is a need for you to reply to any comment or brand mention, do that politely and in a professional manner. Avoid using abusive words. Many of these mentions are complaints and queries about a product, so take time to read them and provide answers and solutions to concerns raised.

Retweeting

Retweeting is an acceptable practice and so feel free to do it. It is a veritable means of solidifying your leadership in the app field.

Use favorite tweets to get the attention of a follower

Favoriting tweets is as effective and efficient –if not more efficient and effective – as retweeting in getting the attention of a follower.

Follow and connect trends and hashtags to your app

Your marketing strategy on Twitter will become more effective if you follow hashtags and trending topics. However, you should look for a way to connect your app and brand with the trending topics, as this will make more people see your handle when they perform searches on trending topics and hashtags.

Give special promotion deals and discounts to your followers

A good means of getting more followers and making your current followers keep retweeting you is to launch contests with some impressive prizes such as coupons and discounts. The contest can be having people post photos of themselves using your apps. Just be creative in initiating the contest.

Get visual

The use of images and videos in social media marketing has proved to be effective. In fact, research has shown that more clicks, shares, downloads and views are obtained from photos, images and videos than from plain text. So, incorporate images and videos in your tweets. However, it has to be images that are relevant to your app or niche

Promoted tweets can do the tricks

Use promoted tweets to reach your target audience directly. In this way, you avoid wasting your time and money on an uninterested audience. If you are using promoted tweets, aim at giving value to your audience. Thus, ensure that you are not providing them with spammy tweets.

Integrate your Twitter with your other marketing activities outside the platform

You can make your marketing much more effective by incorporating it into other marketing activities that you are engaged in. For example, if you are running a contest on Twitter, it will be good that you let your fans on the other social media platforms you are using know about your Twitter contest. You can also let the visitors to your blog to be aware of the contest.

Use Twitter analytics in finding out what is trending among your audience

Twitter analytics is a good tool that will help you in your Twitter marketing campaign. You can find out the kind of content your followers like, the best days to post tweets and the demographics of twitter users following you. This data is available on the dashboard of the Twitter analytics. With the data, you will be able to analyze your Twitter marketing campaign, determine what is working and what is not working, and do a revaluation of your posts.

Capture the Instagram Audience

Instagram is another social media platform with a lot of members. It is a platform where people share photos and images. At its budding stage, businesses were not using it to promote their brand but today it has millions of users and over a million businesses advertising on it. You can also adopt it as a channel of promoting your apps for the following reasons.

Large number of consumers
One of the reasons why you should advertise your apps in Instagram is because of the number of consumers of various kinds of products visiting the platform. There are a lot of business profiles on this platform. Many people come to the social media platform just to find out new products on the market and other things they care about. In other words, there is a huge number of people that also want to discover new apps they can use to accomplish a specific task. This explains why millions of advertisers come to Instagram from different parts of the world to promote their business and share their success stories to consumers. You can join these advertisers to reach out to a lot of consumers. About 60% of consumers on the platform reported that they succeeded in finding new products with the platform. This shows that the platform is quite effective.

Users spend more time on the platform
Advertisers and businesses share videos and images on the platform. Many users of the platform spend more time watching videos and viewing images. According to the study, there is an 80% increase in time spent on video watching on Instagram and many of these videos and images viewed on the platform are from businesses. This shows that ads reach their target audience.

Indeed, Instagram is a great platform for advertising as it uses the demographic data of Facebook to serve ads to the right audience. Check out Instagram success stories in order to be more convinced about the effectiveness of Instagram as a marketing tool.

How to Advertise on Instagram
You can advertise your apps on Instagram in the following manner.

Establishing a community around an actionable hashtag
A very good means of promoting an app on Instagram is to initiate a hashtag campaign and establish a community around it. Many businesses and individual markets have used this method and it worked for them. One advantage of initiating such a campaign is that it can be incorporated into other marketing activities on other social media networks such as Twitter.

Make posts and comments that are relevant to your brand

While relating to your followers on Instagram, it is good that you post comments that are relevant to your brands. One important factor that you should also bear in mind when you are posting on Instagram is the reason why your followers are on the site. They are seeking information that will be useful to them in a fun manner. So, also make posts that are relevant to your brand and your followers. In this way, your followers will come to know more about your product and how it will be of help to them.

Have a sense of humor

Learn how to pass information across to your followers in a humorous manner. Take a clue from conventional advertisers. Many of them captivate their viewers in a fun manner. So, it is not enough to make relevant posts; it is also good that you make it lively and amusing. In this manner you will be able to captivate your followers and make your post fun to read.

Don't kill your marketing campaign with too much posting

It is good that you keep your followers busy by making posts on regular basis, but don't over post, otherwise you may end up annoying them when you clog their feeds. Experience has shown that too much posting can result in the loss of followers. It is not uncommon to see people unsubscribe because they feel that their feeds are being clogged up with pictures. Ideally, don't post more than 2 times per day in this platform. If it is important that you post multiple pictures, you can make use of the album feature of Instagram. A lot of Instagram users are not aware of this feature because it was released in February 2018.

Popularize your Instagram on other social media platforms

Add your Instagram icons on your website and also include links to your Instagram bio page on other social media networks that you belong to. Before you create an account on Instagram, it is advisable that you first connect it with Facebook so that you can bring in your friends from Facebook to the platform.

Utilize the marketing features of Instagram

If you are new to Instagram, take time to learn more about the social media platform. There are a lot of marketing tools on the platform and it is being updated on regular basis. So, if you are using the platform to promote your app, it is good that you use all the marketing features it comes with. Indeed, there are a lot of things that you can do on Instagram in order to make your marketing campaign more effective and efficient. For example, you can track performance and edit your photos to improve their look on the Platform. Some of the tools in the platform that may be useful to you include profile views, impressions, website clicks, email clicks, call clicks, reach, gender breakdown, top locations, age range, stay Insta-smart and others.

Learn from others

There were other businesses and app developers marketing on Instagram before you joined. Some of these developers and businesses have an excellent grasp of the features of Instagram and how to market on it. Go through their pages and posts and see if you can learn one or two things from them. Incorporate their ideas into your marketing strategy. Besides businesses and developers marketing on the platform, you should also get inspiration from your followers and learn from them.

Let people know how your app can add value to the world and change their lives

Initiate a campaign aimed at showing how your followers can improve their lives with your app and what the world will gain from it. You also need to show how you as a developer view the world and how you can make it better with your apps. However, your impression of the world should be meaningful to your followers.

Be active on the platform

Many people make the mistake of concentrating solely on posting to their followers but they don't interact with other Instagram users. It is not enough to get people to follow you; it is also important that you follow others. Search for trending hashtags especially in your category and contribute to them. Make comments on other people's posts. You can also regram a photo but don't forget to acknowledge the source. If you are targeting an account, it is a good thing that you subscribe for notifications that show whenever there is a new post on the account.

Instagram advertising options

Currently, the platform is offering 4 ad options. Find out the features of each option and see which one is the best option for you. Here are the various advertising options of Instagram:
- Stories ads

- Carousel ads
- Video ads
- Photo ads.

Reach Internet Users via Blogging

As mentioned above, it is good that you use social media platforms together with other Internet marketing strategies and one of such strategies is blogging. Blogging is an easy and affordable means of increasing the popularity of your app online and also increasing the visibility of your website. It could be regarded as a traditional means of promoting a product on the Internet. It will also be good that you include it in your marketing strategy.

What is a blog?

Briefly put, a blog is a website that a person or a business uses to share information, opinions or discuss various topics on their niche. Readers or visitors to the blog are permitted to comment on the posts by the blog owners as a way of contributing to the discussion.

Marketing your app in a blog: Tips

Here are tips to help you promote your apps in a blog.

Set up a posting schedule and general topics to deal with

Just as with social media platforms, it is also good that you post often on your blog so that your readers will always find something new whenever they visit your blog. It is not uncommon to see blogs with the most recent posts made more than one month in the past. This is not good practice. It is good that you have a good schedule for posting on your blogs. You should also decide on the topics to be discussed on your blog.

What to do with in your content

In blogging, you have total control over your content. Unlike social media channels, you are the master here and there are no rules to follow except the ones you set for yourself when it comes to deciding on the type of content to post. If you want to get the best from this marketing strategy, here are issues to address in your content:

1. Write content that promotes your products.

2. Write content that provides tips, guidelines and advice to the readers. In this way, your readers will see you as an expert in the field, especially if they find your tips and solutions very helpful.
3. Provide your readers with content that tells them how your app is useful to them.
4. Share your company's experiences and stories with them.
5. Provide answers and solutions to your readers' questions and concerns about your content. Many people visit a blog in order to ask questions on an aspect of the blogger's brand. So, when you receive any question from a reader, make sure that you reply quickly.
6. If you have received any award in the past or present on any of your apps, it is also good that you publicize it on your blog.

Creating your content with the right keyword
It is good that you optimize your content with the right keywords. Your blogging effort will amount to an exercise in futility if you don't use the right keywords, especially if you want to improve your visibility with blogging. Use Google Insights to find popular keywords in your niche.

Submit your blog to relevant search engines
You are likely going to get a lot of clicks if you optimize your content with the right keywords and then submit the URL of your blog to popular search engines such as Google, Yahoo, Bing and Technorati. In some of these search engines, you will not be charged to submit the URL of your blog.

Link your posts to other blogs in the same niche as you
You don't have to be selfish in blogging. Sometimes, you become popular by promoting other people's posts. You have to take time to read the blogs of your competitors. If you see any interesting article that is relevant to your niche, you can comment on that and then provide a link to your blog in your comment where readers can find more information on the topic. A good number of people that read your comment will definitely click on your link to find more information on the topic of discussion. In this way, you lure visitors to another person's blog to your blog. Don't forget to set a pingback or trackback when you link in order to let the blog owner know that you have linked to their blog.

Get involved in guest posting

Look for a popular blog that deals with similar topics to you. If you find one, contact the owner to see if you can guest post with them. Many well-known blogs provide opportunities for guest posting because they have a need for new posts with new ideas. You should also request the blog owner to post in your blog as well.

Incorporate other social media platforms into your blog

As is the case with social media, it is also good that you incorporate social media platforms in your blog. Don't forget to include links to your bios and profile pages. In this way, your readers will visit your social media pages if they are interested in your topic.

Invest in Social Media Management Tools

As I have advised above, it is important that you have a presence in all the major social media networks to make your social media marketing more effective. Fortunately, a lot of social media marketing tools have been introduced to help social media managers run effective marketing campaigns on various platforms and manage multiple accounts easily. It will be good that you invest in these social media management tools. Here are some popular ones to use:

1. Hootsuite
2. Buffer
3. IFTTT
4. SocialOomph
5. TweetDeck
6. Tweepi
7. ArgyleSocial
8. SocialFlow
9. SproutSocial
10. SocialBro
11. Crowdbooster
12. DashBurst.

Popularize Your Brand with Display Advertising

Display advertising, also known as banner advertising, is a veritable means of letting many app consumers both online and offline know about your app. It is a means of promoting a product visually using logos, text, videos, animations, photographs, graphics and the likes. It is available in two forms: online display advertising and offline. The latter includes the use of banners, billboards, stickers, lettering, printed texts and the likes for commercial purposes. This kind of display advertising is good for app developing companies and individual developers that have offline bases. However, if you operate online more, you should use more of Internet display advertising. Here, we will concentrate more on online banner advertising.

Generally, in display banner advertising, advertisers target consumers with specific traits. The adverts are placed on third party sites. The commercial messages, in video, image or text form, can also be posted on social media sites like Facebook. You can see such advertising in search engine results as well as in emails. Internet display advertising simply means posting your commercial messages on a third party's website known as a publisher and you are charged for the space occupied by your ads. The success of this marketing campaign depends to a considerable extent on the publisher you choose. It is important to use a popular publisher that will help you spread the news about your app to the app users. So, if you are going to use this method of advertising, it is important that you consider the following factors when choosing a publisher.

The stats of a publisher
Before you choose a publisher, you should take time to go through their stats. There are some online tools like Alexa.com that will provide you with a lot of information on a publisher. Check the number of visitors the publishers have on a monthly basis, the location of these visitors (this is very important in case your target audience is people from a particular location) and the demographics of the visitors (this is also very important for app developers that are targeting a particular set of people, gender, age or people in a particular works of life).

Does the publisher promote apps?
Another important question to ask before choosing a publisher is the type of ads or content being promoted by the publisher. You want to promote your apps, so it will make no sense to use a publisher that promotes fashion accessories or any other kinds of items other than apps and software.

The frequency at which you can update your ads

Each publisher has rules and regulations guiding advertising on their websites. Some allow advertisers to update ads whenever they want, while some don't tolerate that. It is important that you take this factor into consideration before you choose a publisher so that you will not have any reason to complain if there are such restrictions.

Find out where your competitors are advertising

It is likely that your competitors, especially those that have been in app development for many years before you, have carried out a thorough research on display advertising and publishers in the industry before choosing one. The implication of this is that they are using the right publisher with a good reputation. You too can make use of the same publishers they are using in order to gain what they are gaining. However, this does not mean you will not search for better advertisers. You can try finding out how successful your competitors have been with their publishers by using a competitive intelligence.

With the above tips, you will be able to find a reliable display advertising publisher to hire to advertise your ads for you on their platform.

Pay-per-Click Advertising

Thousands of businesses and individuals are promoting their products and brand via pay-per-click advertising. While many of them have directed a lot of traffic to their websites through it, others gained nothing from it. The truth is that to successfully promote your app via pay-per-click advertising, you need to have a deep knowledge of how the method works. Your PPP effort will definitely yield huge traffic that will finally convert if you get every step of it right. But the opposite will be the case if you fail to get every detail right regardless of how small it is. Apply these tips in your pay-per-click marketing campaign for the popularization of your app.

Learn the meaning of pay-per-clicking

If you have not heard of pay-per-click advertising, I would suggest that you take time to read about it. It is not within the scope of this book to provide detailed information about this method of advertising. Here, I will only provide you with tips on how to use it. But how can you use what you don't know what it is all about? This is why I suggest that you take time to learn about what it is and how it works so that you will be able to appreciate it fully.

State your objectives

Now that you have known what PPC is all about, the next thing to do is set your goals or objectives. The basic question to ask yourself here is what you will want to achieve through this kind of advertising. Are you trying to get people to download your app? Do you want to drive traffic to your website? Do you want viewers of the advert to subscribe to your newsletter? You need to have a clear objective, as you are going to assess the campaign based on the extent these objectives are met. Besides, it is your objective that will determine the keywords you will choose. The message of your advert will also reflect your objectives.

Choose a search engine

Virtually all search engines have pay-per-click advertising programs. However, due to the difference in the popularity of search engines, these PPC programs do not give the same result. I will advise you to choose any of the PPC programs of any of the popular search engines, which include Google AdWords, Bing Ads or Yahoo! Gemini. Find out the requirements for setting up sponsored advertising, as it is also called, and then follow the instructions in order to start running the campaign.

Choose your keywords or key phrases

I have already provided you with tips on how to choose a keyword. The tips discussed apply here as well. I need to emphasize here that the keywords you will use should be what consumers normally search for in the search engine when they are looking for information on your product. Use abbreviations and synonyms to diversify your keyword range.

Make your budget

PPC is not a free type of advertising. It is something that you have to spend on, but advertisers are charged per click. Before you register for the program, it is important that you first decide the amount you will be willing to pay for any click. You can start from a small amount and then increase later when you start getting a good return on investment. When deciding on the size of your budget, you should consider your overall marketing budget, the likely ROI and the competitiveness of your market. For example, if you budget 5% of your selling price on advert, you should determine what percentage of that amount you will be spending on per click using conversion rates.

Write a compelling advert
There is always a short advert to which your PPC link will be attached. This advert should have a title and a body. You have to professionally write it, focusing on your marketing objectives. It should be persuasive so that after reading it, an app user cannot but click on the link. In case you are not good in writing, you can hire an expert freelancer writer to write it for you.

Help your client to take the next step
It will be good to assist your potential consumer to make a decision and take the next step you will want them to take. So, you should have a landing page, which should be well optimized with the relevant keywords. It is not good practice to direct a customer to your website's homepage. Your landing page should describe your app using text and images. It should also include prices and a click to buy button as well as your contact details. With these pieces of information, your would-be client will be well guided.

Keep track of everything
The beauty of PPC is that you will be able to know where you are spending your money, the amount you've spent and the amount the marketing campaign is earning you. You should also be able to find out how each keyword is performing in the campaign. As you will be trying different keywords and methods, it will be important that you keep track of every aspect of the marketing campaign. Always bear in mind what your PPC marketing objectives are to sell your app. By keeping track of everything, you will find out the keywords that are not bringing enough sales and then remove them, especially the important ones. Don't make blind decisions. Use data you obtain from your track record to make decisions that will improve performance. Apart from keywords, you should also keep track of the location of your users or where you are getting more users, how they are interacting with your site and the rate at which they convert to sales.

Incorporate search engine optimization into your PPC campaign
Though PPC is an effective means of marketing and promoting an app or any other product, you can make it more effective by incorporating search engine optimization into it. With the combination of these

marketing strategies, as well as other marketing strategies explained above, your website will surely occupy a prominent position in search engine results. You will also have the same experience in your paid ads.

Enlarge your budget as your ROI is increasing
I advised above that you should have a budget. This budget should not be static as I mentioned. It should vary depending on your ROI. So, if you are making more returns on investment, you have to increase your budget in order to make more returns. You don't have to increase your budget arbitrarily. You can monitor your success and increase when it is obvious that you are succeeding in the campaign.

Note that PPC is like an investment, so when going into it, see it as a long-term plan. Initially, it may not be yielding any profit. During the budding stage of the campaign, you will be spending on the campaign trying different strategies, testing copies and landing pages. With time, you will discover the best formula that will help you to make more sales.

Promote Your App on Your Site
I have spent time discussing various ways to popularize and market an app. This discussion would be bereft of completeness if I failed to mention ways you can promote your app on your website. There is the tendency to talk about all ways to market an app except through a website, but the truth is your website presents you with plenty of opportunities to advertise your product.

Building a website
The first step to take is to create a powerful and nice looking website. Make sure that your website has rich content that is well-optimized with relevant keywords. The content should also be relevant to your targeted audience. By this, I mean that the website should be for the app. Besides the social media channels, there is no other avenue of showcasing the real value of your app except through your website. Besides, it is a great platform for connecting to your would-be users and providing them with a sound and convincing reason why they should download your app.

Create a landing page for your app in your website
I have already talked about the uses and importance of having a well optimized landing page above. Suffice it to mention here that they are

great avenues of telling your potential customers about your app, its features and then persuading them to purchase it or to click to download it. Put differently, a landing page is the marketing page of your website.

Optimize your app's website

It is not enough to create a website; you need to have a landing page and fill it with content. You need to also invest in search engine optimization. As I earlier mentioned, it does to a website what App store optimization does to an app page in an app store. If you don't have a good SEO service and strategy, there is no need investing in a website, as nobody will find it. There is no better way of making app users discover your app on your website than through organic search traffic. This is why you have to optimize your website.

Build a press kit for media coverage

You should target not just consumers of your app but also influencers and other secondary audiences in your promotion. To ensure that you get them, it is important that you build an app press kit so that journalists and influencers who have questions to ask about your app can easily do that. Journalists or freelancers may want to write about your app and they don't know what it is all about. Through this feature, they can contact you and ask you questions regarding that. Make sure that you have your promotional material to share with them if they have an interest in your product. Creating a press kit is not a difficult task. Search on Google or any other popular website and you will obtain helpful tips on how to create one.

Show your website's visitors that you have an app by including GoogBarber promote widgets in your website. Use the single link in GoogBarber to link to your app. Users that click on this link will be directed to the app store where you are selling your app regardless of the platform they are browsing with.

Make sure that your website has a Smart App Banner designed for the promotion of iOS apps on websites. This feature was released with iOS6.

Chapter 5: App Monetization Models

In chapters 3 and 4, I talked about how to plan and execute an app marketing campaign plan. Now, I should tell you various ways you can monetize your app apart from the normal downloads from users. It is good that you learn about these monetization models, as it will help to increase the revenue you generate from your app. Consequently, in this chapter, I am going to discuss the various ways of monetizing your apps.

In-app Ads

If you want your app to generate more funds for you outside the money you will raise from selling your app directly or indirectly to the users, the first app monetization model to consider is in-app ads. It is simply what it sounds like; it is a means of generating more money by putting advertisements in your app page. However, it needs to be professionally done otherwise the ads can annoy visitors to your mobile app page. Here are some tips to help you get it right with this app monetization method.

Align your app to the users' interest
One important factor to bear in mind is the user experience. It is good that you create ads that are in line with the interest of the users. In this way, you add value to your clients' experience and improve on your app. Always think of how the ad will pop up in your app. Put yourself in the place of the users and see how you will feel with the flow of the ads in your app. Is the interference with experience or usage of the app very annoying? Do you like the look of the ads and the performance of your app as well as the experience you are getting when the ads are popping up? Are you happy with the placement of the ads on the app? If the answers to the questions are negative, then it is likely that your users will not like the ads.

Ideally, the ads should be properly placed in the app in such a manner that they appear as natural parts of the entire platform. For example, for a gaming app, it will make sense if the ads pop out after a break or at the end of the level before the beginning of another level.

Another important factor to take into consideration is the frequency at which the ads come out or the number of times your user will see the ads. It is not good to bore them with too many ads. If there are too many ads coming out at a close interval, the user of the app will lose interest in them. Once they have no interest in the ads, they will no longer be clicking on them and their appearance will begin to infuriate them. Set a limit to the number of ads that you display to users on a daily, weekly and monthly basis.

Make your app part of the experience of native ads

I have already made this point above but it is good that I highlight it here. Create a personalized ad that matches your app in all aspects. It should look like a natural part of the app. Custom ads are the type that you are able to determine their location, size, look and feel. The messages they carry are compelling. With their look, size and placement, you are most likely going to earn more money from them. Though a native ad should appear like a natural part of the app, it should be properly demarked or separated from the rest of the app content. Other clickable buttons or features in the app should also stand at a good distance from the app. In this way, users will not mistakenly click on the ads or another feature.

Guide against accidental ad clicks

There is nothing that annoys users more than clicking on an ad when they actually don't want to. This also will affect you in a way. Besides, he or she will not take any action expected by the advertiser. The ad will get many clicks but little revenue, as the effectiveness of an ad is measured based on whether or not users take the required action. Here are ways of guiding against accidental clicks:

- Don't place ads over images, text and other clickable features.
- Create a large and conspicuous call to action button.
- Ensure that users differentiate ads from other features. You can achieve this by labeling the ad.
- Select a network for your ads and ensure that its network SDK is updated.

Freemium Model

The freemium model is a method of monetizing an app by offering a limited or stripped down version of the app free of charge and then selling the premium features. There is the tendency for some people to think that freemium is just like giving out chaff for free and selling the main seed. If you have such a mind set, you have to think twice. The basic idea of this model is to offer a free sample to users so that they can see what the app is all about even when they have not gotten it all. So, the one you are giving out freely has to be properly done so that users will be happy with the quality or the experience they obtain from its usage. The positive experience they have will make them go for the premium features or added services.

Freemium apps are available in a number of types, which include the following:

- Classic, feature-limited freemium in which users are allowed to utilize limited features of the app free of charge.

- Free trial period, which allow users to use all the features of the app for a limited duration.

- Ads and sponsored content in which a free app is monetized with sponsored content and ads.

- Freemium plus paid app in which the developer offers both freemium and paid app.

Regardless of the type you want to offer, don't forget to improve on users' experience. Remember that it is given for free in order to entice more users or to encourage users to pay for the real app. So, if they don't have a rewarding experience, they will not pay for the main app.

Tips for running an effective freemium campaign

If you want to monetize your app with freemium, take the following points into consideration:

- Create an app that users will love and that will give them a rewarding experience.
- Offer users a good reason to upgrade by restricting the number of features that they can access, for example. Don't give out all

the important features free of charge. Allow them to use only the basic features.
- Include ads and sponsored content following the tips given above as means of increasing your revenue.

Make Money with Your App Via Affiliates and Referrals

Affiliate marketing is a veritable means of monetizing your apps or increasing the revenue you generate from it. Affiliate marketing is allowing other people to help you market and sell your app. You will pay them commission for any download of your app that comes through their affiliate link. It is an effortless and cost-effective way of promoting and selling your app. The affiliate members know that the amount of money they will make depends on the number of downloads coming via their affiliate links. So, they will naturally put in more effort in order to sell more and make more money. The implication of this is that you will relax and be getting revenues from different sources.

However, it has to be well done for this objective to be achieved. If you want to run an affiliate program, your app should of great quality, otherwise you will end up not achieving anything. Nobody likes to waste time marketing a product that consumers will not purchase. High selling apps, on the contrary, will attract more affiliate marketers.

Affiliate programs are similar to referral programs. The referral strategy is exactly what it sounds like. You pay people a stipulated percentage of the amount of money spent on your app by any person they refer to your app store. Any person that wants to participate in the program is assigned a unique link, which helps you to keep track of sales coming from each member. It is left for you to decide whether to pay commission on any product purchased by a referred customer or to pay a fixed amount. No matter how you want to pay your affiliate, always give them what is due to them and keep for yourself an amount that will not cause you any loss. The end point of any affiliate and referral program is to help you generate more money. You don't have to run a loss via the method. However, don't pay peanuts as your commission.

In-App Purchases

This monetization strategy is quite similar to freemium. Some people consider it as a type of freemium. But here, I prefer to treat it briefly as a separate monetization model. It is commonly used in gaming apps. In this model, you allow gaming enthusiasts to play your games free of charge. However, if they want to win any prize during the play, they have to pay some money. Just as in freemium, always give your users reasons to make purchases. They will surely spend on the paid content if they find value in it.

Chapter 6: Selling Your Apps

This chapter brings us to the third section of this book, which is how to sell an app. If you create an app, you need to promote, popularize and then sell it to app users to make money from it. How do you determine the price to sell your app at? What are the app stores you can sell your app in? How are you going to sell it? These are some of the crucial questions that I will answer in this chapter.

How to Determine the Amount to Sell Your App For

When you want to sell your app, you will surely want to sell it at the right price and make some gains. Nobody would want to under sell their apps. To make a reasonable profit from the sale of your app, you should at least have an idea of what your app's value is. This is the highest amount any consumer will be willing to spend on it. If you sell it above this figure, you cheat the buyer and if you sell it below this price, you underestimated your app. The question is, how do you estimate your app's cost? Here are some tips to help you get started.

Calculate your net cash

The first thing to do is to sum up all the money generated by your app and all the expenses you incurred so far in relation to your app starting from the time of its creation to date. Expenses should include app store fees, maintenance and updating costs, licensing costs, development costs and costs for all subscriptions concerning the app. Make sure you include all service costs, even if you are the person that executed the service. This is because you would have paid for the service and save your time. Time is money. Revenue should include download fees and also money made through other monetization models you are using. Subtract your income from your expenses.

Convert your net cash into your app value

Use multiples to determine the cost of your app. There are a number of factors that will determine the multiples to use, however most people multiply their net cash by 2 or 3 to get the value of their app. Here are factors to be taken into consideration when determining the multiple to use:

- Growth prospect: What is the future for your app? This is the major question to consider here. If your app is likely to gain more downloads in the future, then you should use higher multiples. A higher growth prospect means that the app is likely to generate more money in the future. The buyer will still make enough money from it.

- Your app genre/niche: You should take the niche of your app into consideration. This is because apps in some genre have higher growth or are more competitive than others. It is also the niche that determines how an app is regulated.

- Time spent on the app: Another important point that you should factor in here is how much time you put into your app. If you spend a lot of time on your app, the multiple should be higher as well.

- Marketing methods: You should not forget the marketing strategies you are going to use. This is because some are more time-consuming and more expensive than others. Besides, with some, your product will become more popular among consumers.

Taking note of what competing apps were sold for

Another method of determining the price to sell your app at is to find out what amount similar and competing apps were sold for. However, if you are going to use this method, bear in mind that each app is unique. Thus, the fact that an app similar to yours was sold for $10m for example, does not mean that you will sell your app for that price. You can sell yours at a higher or lower price depending on the factors mentioned above. However, knowing the price for which a competitor sold their app will give you an idea of the amount to sell yours at. The important point is that you should be realistic when fixing the selling price of your app. Remember what I said the value of your app is – the highest amount an individual will be willing to spend in its acquisition. Put yourself in the shoes of the buyer. If you were the buyer, could you pay the amount you value it at. If you think you would spend such an amount on the app as a buyer, you value it rightly. Be realistic.

Note that some app marketplaces have launched tools that will enable you to value your app. A typical example of such a platform is MyAppValue built by Apptopia. It is available for free, so you can also use the platform to find out the cost of your app. There may be other app stores that offer such services. If you use this platform, a link to a detailed report showing the breakdown of your app will be emailed to you. The report will contain information about ranks, reviews, app sales, downloads, engagements and ads of your app.

App Marketplace to Sell Your Apps

Selling an app is not a very big deal, as there are many platforms you can sell it on. Some of the platforms are brokerages, while some work like a marketplace or store that brings buyers and sellers together. Here are some of the popular ones that you can use in case you are still in the business.

- *Appbusinessbrokers (*brokerage)

- *AppnGameReskin.com*

- *Apptopia*

- *Sellmyapp*

- *Codester*

- *CodeCanyon.net*

- *Flippa*

- *SellMySourceCode.com*

- *ApkaCode.com*

- *ChupaMobile.com*

- *Apptopia.com*

There are indeed quite a lot of websites where you will be able to sell your app that are not mentioned here. If you ask Google, you will get impressive results.

Promoting Sales with Coupons and Other Promo Deals

Every consumer likes to purchase items at a discounted price. Buyers always support businesses that give them discounts. It is common to see buyers looking for businesses that offer promotion deals in the form of discounts and coupons. App users are looking for great deals, so you can promote sales by incorporating them into your marketing strategy.

Coupons, loyalty programs and others are very effective in mobile app sales. According to a report by Juniper Research, consumers are ten times more likely to use mobile coupons than print coupons. It is now common to find consumers making purchases in offline stores with app loyalty programs and mobile coupons thanks to the rise of in-store proximity payments. You can stimulate conversions and engagement with these promos more than some other campaign strategies. If you are using this kind of strategy, it is of crucial importance that you focus attention on the right audience due to the fact that this type of in-app campaign will require users to spend money.

Using coupons and codes as a means of triggering sales will give you a number of benefits. First, it will help you to grow your fan and custom base. This is because of the reason mentioned above. Consumers normally seek good bargains and move where they find them. Besides, with these promotional deals, it will be easy for you to achieve brand loyalty. App users will always look for your app when they have a need for it because of the discount they will get. Using coupons and promo codes as your marketing strategies will also help you to lead online users to your points of sale. Above all, with these strategies, you will be able to obtain information about the consumers of your app who subscribe for the promotions, as they will have to give some of their personal information such as their email address, name, place of residence, etc. when they are registering for the promo.

If you are going to incorporate coupon and promo codes in your marketing campaign, here are tips to help you do it properly.

Create your coupon image
The first step to take in this regard is to create a customized image of your coupon and promo code. The image should show not just the logo of your brand but also concise details of the promotion. Users who see

the image should know the kind of gift they can purchase with the coupon, the amount of discount offered and other relevant information about it.

Provide guideline and instructions for the coupon use
You should provide clear instructions about the use of the coupon and codes to the participants so that they will know exactly the right line of action to take. The instruction should show all the options and features of the coupon to the participants. This will also help them to make a sound judgment.

Provide the download and save tools
You should incorporate the tools for downloading and saving into your application. With the tools, the users will be able to retrieve and display codes or coupons through PDF, email or printed copy.

Make your coupon compatible with the mobile devices
If you are incorporating coupons and codes into your marketing strategy, it is also essential that you make it compatible with mobile devices. This means making it possible for mobile device users to be able to download, save and retrieve the coupon with their phone. In this way, you will have a campaign in which users will be able to get the coupon from various platforms or from anywhere.

Have a tool for keeping track of users' information
It is important that you have all the information of users that have made use of the coupon codes or that have joined any of promo deal you initiate.

Requesting users to become fans
Coupon and code campaign will help you to grow your fan base. In this respect, you should request users to join your fan page to be able to download the coupon.

Email the promotion code
Your application should have an email platform for automatizing the sending of emails to users following their registration into the promo campaign. Each user should be assigned a unique promotional code, which they will receive via the email. With the email feature, the users can always obtain their codes whenever they check their emails.

Take Note!

If you are incorporating coupons and promo codes in your marketing strategies, it is also good that you be aware of their disadvantages, which include the following:

- Coupons and promo codes can reduce your profit and margins. This is because the discount you give out is part of your profit.
- You may end up having non-loyal shoppers (consumers who are interested in discount only).
- It can make your visitors not purchase your app until the sale period, when they will get discount.
- There is also the possibility of brand damage.

Tracking Your Campaign success

Every marketing campaign should have some objectives or aims. It is also of crucial importance that you take time to find out the extent you have achieved the objectives. This is what is I mean by tracking the campaign success.

You can start by tracking important actions and events. Here, you should put premium on triggered events that are of essence to your app. This can be adding more articles to your news app for readers to read, encouraging users to use app-specific coupon codes in making purchases in your mCommerce app. You can track the following metrics to help you track your campaign success.

Impressions

Impression as a marketing and selling term refers to the number of eyes that view your campaign before triggering the required event. If you are not getting enough impressions or if the number of impressions you have is very small, you have to make an effort to increase your campaign reach.

Click through rate (CTR)

Click through rate is the number of clicks you obtain from every 100 viewers. If you have a high click through rate, it means that users have high interest in your app. What determine the click through rates are design, ad creative and copy, operating systems and displays on different devices. If you are having a low CTR, here are things that you should take into consideration.

- Design performance: One of the causes of low CTR is the design of your ad on in-app messages. Find out how it appears in all devices. If it is blurred or warped when viewed, you will not get enough CTRs.
- Ad copy: Re-evaluate your text and ad copy to ensure that it is compelling. A good ad copy should push readers or users into taking the desired action. So, improve on your text and ad copy to make it more compelling. You can generate more clicks by A/B testing your copy. You can also achieve major results with a simple ad copy just as it can be done via a number of means such as banner ads, email, landing pages.

Conversion Rate

Another important metric to track is the conversion rate, which can be regarded as the standard across-the-board metric, as it is the basic objective of any app campaign. This explains why most of the marketing efforts will finally come down to this. With it you can determine the successful offer and messaging channel. It is possible for you to customize your conversion action and also take measurement of the multiple of each campaign, including downloads as well as checkouts. You will be able to establish three to four conversions in a campaign and then make the analysis of the screen flow, completion rate and drop off metrics in order to measure success.

Note that there are other ways you can keep track of your marketing campaign apart from what has been discussed above. The method to use depends on the marketing strategy you want to track. For example, the way a print and direct mail marketing campaign is tracked is quite different from the way phone calls generated from ads can be tracked. So, list the making methods you used and then find out from Google how you can track it.

Measuring, Repeating Action and Improving Strategy

App marketing strategies and indeed any marketing strategy is not a dogma or something that is so set in stone that it cannot be readjusted or improved on. It is not something that you can establish and then leave it without touching it. Sometimes, it can happen that a campaign that was a failure in the past can give positive results in the future. Consequently, app marketing should be taken as an ongoing effort, which should have multiple channels. You should therefore establish a thoughtful, holistic and thorough approach to marketing, which will result in a better app usage, higher mCommerce revenue and more engaged users. Your marketing campaign is one that will make the user feel that they are having the best possible experience. So, after the initial planning and implementation of your marketing and sell campaign, go back to assess its effectiveness. Whether it is giving the required result or not, think of ways of improving it so that it will give a better result. If there is a need to repeat a marketing campaign, you should not hesitate to do it. Don't just drop a marketing campaign simply because it did not yield the required result for you in the past. Remember, a strategy may be ineffective today but effective tomorrow.

Take Advantages of Google Remarking

It is not every visitor that comes to your website that will eventually download your app, but it is a good marketing strategy to go after these members of your targeted audience who did not make any purchase, as it is still possible to bring them to purchase your app. The method of going after these visitors with the aim of making them purchase or download your app afterwards is what is known as remarketing. This marketing strategy makes it possible for you to bring targeted ads directly to a defined audience that come to your site through other means when they are surfing the Internet. It can be regarded as an affordable means of increasing the popularity of your app and also reminding your visitors to purchase or download your app. I strongly recommend that you incorporate remarketing into your entire marketing campaign if you have a website.

There are basically two major ways of delivering remarking ads: text and image display formats. You can use the two means or use one. The ads are displayed on the websites your targeted audience has visited before and they are managed in Google Adwords.

Benefits of remarketing

It makes sense to make remarketing a part of your entire marketing campaign for a number of reasons or for the benefits you will derive from it. Here are the various ways you will benefit from remarketing.

- Reaching potential users
- Targeting a specific population
- Reaching people via their devices

- Efficient pricing
- Easy for users to locate you
- Getting your campaign statistics
- Easy creation of ads

Methods of Remarketing in Google Adwords

You can remarket with Google Adwords in different ways as explained below.

- **Standard remarketing**: This method allows you to display your ads to the previous visitors to your site as they surf various apps and websites on Display Network.

- **Dynamic remarketing**: It is a method of remarketing which makes it possible for you to include the products and services displayed on your website in the ads you show to your prospective users.

- **Video remarketing:** It targets people that have viewed your videos or YouTube channel when they entered this video sharing platform or when they surf through websites, apps and Display Network videos.

- **Remarketing lists for search ads:** With this method, your ads will be shown to the previous visitors of your site as they look for services or products they require after going through your site.

- **Customer list remarketing:** This method allows you to upload contact information provided by your customer. When people on the contact list login to Google, your ads will be displayed or shown to them regardless of the Google products they are looking for.

Chapter 7: Getting Feedback

After carrying out a successful app marketing campaign and getting users to download your app, it is essential that you find out what your users think about your app. They may be having an impressively positive or annoyingly negative experience with your app. You cannot know this if you have no channels of connecting with them. In marketing and selling apps, there are two major reasons why you should make an effort to obtain feedback from the users of your app. The first is to get more reviews and ratings for your apps and the second is to get an insight into the imperfection of your apps or ways you can improve on it. In this chapter, I am going to discuss the various ways you can obtain feedback on your app.

Before Seeking Feedback

Obtaining feedback from your consumers is much more than getting them to comment on your app or to review your app. There are a number of things you should do first before seeking feedback. Here are the first lines of action to take in this regard.

The first thing you should do is to define your intention of seeking feedback. This is of crucial importance, as it will help you to determine and outline the desired outcome. You should also define the process of getting feedback. It is essential that you outline the process to avoid getting feedback that will not represent the audience fully or that will confuse the understanding of your customers' experience. In order to properly define the process, here are some important questions to ask yourself:

- What are you going to do with the information you will obtain?
- Which channel will be the most suitable for your goals?
- Which aspect of your users' experience are looking to better?

Gathering Feedback via Email

Email is one of the common means of obtaining customers' feedback on your app. This channel may appear to be simple and popular, but not many people get it right. You will be able to enhance the way the users of your app can provide you with feedback via email using a number of methods. These methods increase the efficiency and effectiveness of emails as a channel of getting responses from your customer. If you are requesting feedback via email, there are three essential factors to focus on:

1. You should promise them a quick reply.
2. You should develop a well-articulated system for customer feedback, for example trello.
3. It is of crucial importance that you send a true follow-up emails.

Using Surveys to Get Feedback

Another method you can use to get your users' reply is via a survey. This approach can be somewhat difficult and requires some expertise. It is always a difficult task to create relevant questions to ask the participants in the survey, so it is of crucial importance that you approach the method with utmost care.

You can carry out a survey via the Internet. Survey Monkey is an example of a tool for carrying out a traditional, full-length survey. For a shorter survey, a tool like Qualaroo will be ok. Some of these tools allow users to customize their questions. Whether you are conducting a shorter survey or a longer survey, you should abide by these guidelines:

- Define your end goal and ask questions that will help you to achieve that.
- You should ask open-ended questions that are smartly constructed.
- Don't ask more than one question at a time.
- Create a consistent rating scale.
- Don't ask leading and loaded questions

Usability Tests

Usability tests are more reliable than any other method. The only problem with them is that they require planning in advance. This method takes into consideration imperfections that customers are not aware of or may disregard. Besides, it shows ways to improve on your customer experience or ways of getting rid of the shortcomings of your app. I normally use usability test sin obtaining design details for my apps. If you carry it out very well, you will be able to get right whatever that is lacking in your application.

A usability test is the right method to use for web-based apps and other products that are based on the Internet. In this method, you allow consumers to use your product for free within a specified period of time. The users taking part in this program should have a diary where they will write down their comments based on their experiences. This will give you the opportunity to know and correct the drawbacks of your app before releasing it to the larger public.

Direct interviews with the consumers

A great way of understanding the users of your app and how they feel about your app is to interview them directly. You can carry out the interview online via social media platforms like Facebook. Some of these social media networks have chat and video call features. You may schedule an interview with some of your fans and friends. The interview should be based on their experience of your app. You can also carry out the interview offline, of course.

Pay more attention to the attitude of the users or how they view a problem. Their impression of your app will help you to know features or problems to address.

Use the critical incident method. In this method, you aim at finding out things that work well and those that don't. You have to ask users features they are finding useless and those that they are finding helpful. Ask about how they use your app. Sometimes, some users may not be aware of a problem because they are not using your app correctly or because they are using it in a manner that they are not supposed to.

Use social media to gather information about your product. I have talked about how to use different social media to promote your apps. If you are using this media in the right manner, your friends, fans and followers will be making comments on their experience of your app. Take time to read their comments. From their comments and questions, you will know exactly what they want that they are not getting from your app yet. Apart from reading through their comments, you can also conduct a survey or an interview via these platforms as mentioned above.

Google Analytics

Google analytics will provide you with detailed information about how app users visit your website and what they are doing in your website. You will also find out whether they are downloading your app or not. The users are not talking to you directly but you can find out what their impressions are from their activities in your website.

Include a feedback or comment box in your website. Users of your product can easily leave their feedback after visiting your website if you have a comment or feedback box. Note that it is also possible to include this feature inside your app.

Integrate feedback forms. This simply means that you should custom-build all features for getting reviews and feedback in your entire package. For example, you can build such a feature in the middle of the news feed. The advantage of natively incorporating a feedback form is that it does not irritate anyone like pop-ups do. A user can decide to ignore it or provide answers to the questions asked.

Chapter 8: Ethical Consideration

The marketing and selling of apps and indeed any other type of items should be done with a certain form of morality. You should be sincere and honest in your marketing approach. There shouldn't be any form of deception. This chapter discusses the morality and the best practices to apply when marketing your app.

Honesty and Truth

You become an advertiser as soon as you release your app to the public for download and use. This is because you have to convince app users to download your app rather than that of your competitors. Legally speaking, anything you tell a buyer in order to convince him or her to purchase your product regardless of the medium through which you pass the information can be regarded as an ad. As a rule of the thumb, you should be truthful when talking about your app in any way or channel, whether it is on your website or in an app store. Don't deceive the buyers with false claims or misleading talks. Don't tell your prospective users that your app can do this and that, when in actual fact it cannot do any of them. It is also unethical to intentionally hide important information about your product from the users, especially when revealing such data will make them not purchase your app. It can be interpreted as deception. When talking about your app, bear in mind that you are speaking not just to software and app developers and engineers but also to the unsuspecting public. So, present your app in a manner that ordinary users can understand it. Always provide solid proof to back up any claim you make about your app.

Note that each country has laws guiding advertising. In most jurisdictions, untruthful advertising can be punished by law. So, if you deceive your audience, you may be taken to court by some of them for deception. In the past developers were taken to court by FTC because they failed to bring reliable evidence to back up their claim that their apps can cure acne. This is why I earlier advised you to always provide strong evidence to back up claims about your apps.

Truthful advertising also entails that you disclose clear and unclouded details about your products. This means that the information you are providing in your advertising should be clear, unambiguous and big enough for users to notice and understand them. This applies for print advertising and labeling.

Integrate Privacy Protection into Your Marketing Practices

Nobody will want his or her personal details to be divulged to anyone. Consumers will definitely buy from your competitors if you cannot guarantee them the privacy of their data. Privacy protection entails keeping the data you collect well secured. Privacy protection regulations also oblige you to securely dispose of data and to collect only the needed data. It is a violation of privacy laws to request too much data from your users. You should take the privacy principles into consideration when you are choosing your apps' default settings. Depending on the kinds of app that you want to sell, it is also advisable that you make the default settings consistent with what people would expect.

Always seek the express permission of users if you want to collect or share any information that is not apparent. In this way, your users will not divulge information that they would not want to give out. In the event of any violation of the privacy law, aggrieved customers may take you to court and claim damages. This is why you should be very careful when it comes to the privacy protection of consumers' personal details.

Kids Privacy Protection

Not every app is meant for use by adults. If your app is designed to be used by young people below the age of 13, it is essential that you protect their privacy. There are laws guiding children's privacy in various nations like the Children's Online Privacy Protection Act (COPPA). You need to comply to these regulations in your jurisdiction, especially if your app is the type that collects and shares users' data. You should also abide by extant laws on the protection of kids' privacy if you collect children's data from another source.

You are required to offer a clear explanation of your information practices and also notify their parents about your practices. You should also obtain the permission of their parents before you collect the children's personal information. If there is any third party collecting personal data from your app, you are also required to abide by the above obligation.

Kids' privacy protection rules of many countries like COPPA also oblige you to keep any personal information you obtain from underage people very secure and confidential. Note that each jurisdiction has its own definition of what is covered by the privacy rule. Generally, it covers first and last name, screen name, online contact information, telephone number, address, username, geolocation information or a persistent identifier which can be utilised in tracing a user across various websites over a period of time, serial number, cookie identifier, IP address and others.

User Security Is Important

It is not enough to keep to your privacy policy promises; you should also ensure that data is secured. The law requires you to secure your users' information even if you didn't mention what you will do with their information. Personally, I try to relieve myself of these data security obligations by not collecting personal data if I don't have any specific need for them. You should abide by these practices:

- Request only information that you need.
- Take precautions against common security risks in order to secure data that you collect.
- Restrict access to a need-to-know basis.
- Destroy data that you are no longer in need of.

Conclusion

Thank you for buying this book. I hope it has given you some useful insight into how to make your app a success by marketing and selling it. Just remember that it won't be easy, but if you have a solid idea, it is definitely worth it!

Good luck!

Made in the USA
Middletown, DE
10 August 2018